T·H·E
CATHOLIC
VIRTUES

Dear Kelly:

I know we usually give money on special days like this, but I think the wisdom of this book is much more valuable, it will take you a lifetime to spend. If you can follow these Virtues, I'll know my job as your sponsor was successful. Charlie

T · H · E
CATHOLIC
VIRTUES

Seven Pillars of a Good Life

MITCH FINLEY

Liguori

LIGUORI, MISSOURI

Published by Liguori Publications
Liguori, Missouri
http://www.liguori.org

Library of Congress Cataloging-in-Publication Data

Finley, Mitch
    The Catholic virtues : seven pillars of a good life / Mitch Finley.
        p.   cm.
    ISBN 0-7648-0487-1 (pbk.)
    1. Virtues. 2. Catholic Church—Doctrines. I. Title.
BV4630.F46   1999
241'.4—dc21   99–30497

Printed in the United States of America
03 02   5 4 3

DEDICATION

This book is for Michael Leach,
man of faith—not to mention
all the other virtues—gifted publisher,
constant source of encouragement
for those whose written words find their way
to his desk from the four corners of the map,
and a stand-up guy. Thank you, Mike.

ACKNOWLEDGMENTS

My humble gratitude to God for the gift of my Catholic faith, the greatest treasure in my life and the source of endless meaning and joy, however poorly I live its virtues.

Thanks to my spouse, Kathy Finley, for being my number-one exemplar of the Catholic virtues. Thanks to our sons—Sean, Patrick, and Kevin—for teaching me more about God and how to be a Catholic than they could ever imagine.

Contents

INTRODUCTION

I n the late 1950s and early 1960s one of the most popular singing groups in the United States was the Kingston Trio, three young men—Dave Guard, Bob Shane, and Nick Reynolds—who repackaged folk music in a way that had wide appeal. So popular was the Kingston Trio that to this day it is the only group, other than the Beatles, to have had four LP albums simultaneously on *Billboard* magazine's top ten list—and the Trio did it first.

Dave Guard, the Kingston Trio's acknowledged spokesman, was known for his witty between-songs quips. During the Trio's live performances, Guard's amusing patter kept audiences in stitches. He remarked, for example, about a guy who used a cologne that was so manly "it comes in hairy bottles."

Virtue means "manly." The Latin *virtus* literally translates as "manliness," although of course, we cannot limit the capacity for virtue to men, much less men who are so manly they use cologne that comes in hairy bottles. Rather, virtue refers to moral strength regardless of sex; it has to do with inner character, the capacity to live what you say you believe. Virtuous persons are strong, not necessarily in a physical sense but in the sense that they are able to act in a virtuous manner in the face of determined opposition, persecution, or—even more difficult—living in a culture frequently characterized by radical moral relativism, even indifference to right or wrong, good or evil.

Mae West was one of the most popular movie stars of the 1930s and a flamboyant sex symbol. She was famous for her come-hither remark to various men: "Come on up and see me sometime." There are many amusing anecdotes about Mae West, like this one, for example:

> "Goodness, Mae," said a friend, on greeting her, "where did you get those beautiful pearls?"
>
> "Never mind," said Mae, "but you can take it from me that goodness had nothing to do with it."[1]

The character Mae West played, even in her private life, wanted nothing to do with virtue, because when she talked about virtue it was virtue in the worst sense of the word. For the melodramatic Mae, a virtuous person was a puritanical person, a party pooper, a spoil sport. On the contrary, by a virtuous person we mean one who is capable of embracing life and living it to the full. Indeed, we will insist that only the genuinely virtuous person is capable of enjoying life, because the virtuous person finds the mystery of joy and love in all created things.

To focus more directly on the topic of this book then, the Catholic virtues are ways to live a life of moral excellence and goodness according to standards set by the gospel of Jesus and the living tradition of the Catholic Church. According to traditional Catholic teaching, there are two kinds of virtues. First, there are the "theological virtues," which pertain to our relationship with God. Second, there are the "cardinal virtues," from the Latin, *cardo*, which means "hinge"—because these virtues are of foremost importance, which is actually the first dictionary meaning of the term *cardinal*. Everything "hinges" on these virtues in the sense that all other virtues, except the theological virtues, in some way derive from these.[2]

The theological virtues are faith, hope, and love. The cardinal virtues are prudence, justice, fortitude, and temperance. The theological and cardinal virtues are by no means mere abstractions; rather, they reflect an understanding of human nature that takes seriously our tremendous capacity for both good and evil. From a Christian perspective, to cultivate the theological and cardinal virtues is to become Christlike. To consciously make room for the opposite of the virtues, which are vices, is to cultivate self-destruction.

We may find the opposite of a life based on virtue in the traditional list of the seven deadly sins: pride, covetousness, lust, anger, gluttony, envy, and sloth. Although these seven sins are not mirror opposites of the virtues, a life open to them is incompatible with a life based on the cultivation of virtue.

What, then, is a virtue? We may define a virtue as "a way of behaving that makes people and their actions good." To act in a virtuous manner is to fulfill the true purpose of our life. In this sense, to be virtuous is to cultivate and nourish our true self, our deepest self that is destined for eternal union with God, now and in the life to come.

Probably the best known popular theologian of the true self was Thomas Merton, the great twentieth-century American Trappist monk and author. Merton wrote:

> Ultimately the only way I can be myself is to become identified with Him in whom is hidden the reason and fulfillment of my existence.

Therefore there is only one problem on which all my existence, my peace and my happiness depend: to discover myself in discovering God. If I find Him I will find myself and if I find my true self I will find Him.[3]

Here is a great mystery: only by becoming identified with God can we become our own deepest and truest selves, and only if we find our true selves can we find God. The two go together, and the path to both is along the path of virtue. To cultivate the theological and cardinal virtues is to choose both our true selves and union with God, hence their vital importance in the Christian life.

Now, obviously, we don't "gain" a virtue; a virtue does not become part of who we are by some external means. We don't waltz down to the "virtues store" and pick up a box or bag of faith or justice or hope. Rather, we gain a virtue by practicing behaviors associated with that virtue. We become people of faith by acting as if we have faith—and before we know it, we *have faith*. We become hopeful people by acting as if we have hope, and by acting hopeful we *become hopeful*. If we want to be virtuous persons we act virtuously. It's as simple—and difficult—as that. By practicing virtuous behavior we develop virtuous habits, and we become virtuous persons. Therefore the virtues express what we have become on the deepest level.

To practice a virtue, of course, we must know what is good and what is not. We need to make the effort to understand what is good in a particular set of circumstances. This is why the efforts of parents, schools, and society to help children become good persons are vitally important. Only if children grow up knowing how to distinguish between good and evil, right and wrong, will virtuous behavior—and therefore good people—characterize the behavior of society in general.[4]

In other words, virtue is not merely a private concern, a kind of personal hobby some people may choose to pursue while others do not. Rather, the future of the world depends on virtuous persons. The survival of the earth depends on it being populated by people who, from any religious or philosophical perspective, cultivate the cardinal virtues. Prudence, for example, enables us to apply our knowledge of the good to particular situations. Justice maintains appropriate relationships within the community, whether that community be the family, the city, the country, or the world. Fortitude, or courage, regulates fear, aversion, and aggressiveness. Temperance regulates our sensual desires, its proper goal being not asceticism but moderation.[5]

Although the cardinal virtues constitute the minimum for a good life on a human level, they are not enough— not if life in union with our Creator is what we have in mind. Such a life is possible only if we also cultivate the theological virtues of faith, hope, and love. Faith brings us into a loving relationship with God. Hope enables us to act and live as if this relationship with God is real. Love—or "charity," from the Latin, *caritas*—enables us to love God because God is lovable, and to love ourselves and others for the sake of God.

All this may seem too abstract, too theoretical, too out of touch, with the lives of ordinary people. But keep in mind Thomas Merton's concept of the true self. The true self is our deepest reality, the core of who we are and who we want to become. Our deepest center, our true self, is where loving intimacy with God and other people is possible and where it happens. Our true self is what survives death. On a daily basis, our true self lives not in response to the expectations of other people or the dominant culture; not in response to "what's popular," but in response to God's own life, or grace, present and active in the human heart.

When we talk about the Catholic virtues—the theological virtues of faith, hope, and love, and the cardinal virtues of prudence, justice, fortitude, and temperance—we talk about the center of everyday life and our ongoing union with God in that ordinary life. Our focus is on how to be fully Christian and fully human, and therefore we are talking about how to have a life worth living, a life worth getting out of bed for in the morning. We are talking about a life that leaves behind superficiality and embraces, on a deeper level, the Divine Mystery that makes the constellations spin through space, that puts the wiggles, giggles, and cries in a baby which puts joy in the heart of the baby's parents as they watch those wiggles, giggles, and wipe away the tears. To live in loving intimacy with the Divine Mystery and with one another is the purpose of a virtuous life.

This is the goal of our discussion and celebration of the Catholic virtues—to learn more about how to have a life worth living by living in loving intimacy with God, other people, and the earth as our home. This is what the theological and cardinal virtues are all about. This is why reflection on these virtues is a worthwhile occupation.

T·H·E
CATHOLIC
VIRTUES

ₑ

THE VIRTUE
OF FAITH

Words from the Letter to the Hebrews whisper
in our thirsty hearts, probably the best
known words ever written about faith. Listen: "Now faith is the assurance of things hoped for, the
conviction of things not seen" (11:1).

Wondrous words and true—but faith is so great a
mystery that there is no end to understanding it. Faith, to
borrow from an old gospel song, is "so deep you can't
get under it, so high you can't get over it, so wide you
can't get around it, you gotta come in by the door." The
only way to know faith is to embrace faith. True enough,
faith is all that the Letter to the Hebrews says it is. But
faith is so much more.

AUTHENTIC FAITH

For the Hebrew Scriptures, faith (*aman*—to be firm, solid,
and, therefore, true) is "a personal relationship with the
God on whose strength and absolute sureness we can literally stake our lives."[1] The God in whom the Old Testa-

1

ment puts its faith is the God who liberates the Israelites from servitude in Egypt, who speaks through the prophets, and who inspires the author(s) of the Psalms to sing his praises and beg for his mercy.

In the New Testament, faith (Greek, *pisteuein*) refers, above all, to our relationship with the risen Christ, who claims from each of his followers the complete surrender to him that the Hebrew people gave to the Lord God.[2] Faith in the Lord Jesus means turning around our entire existence in dedication to him, and finding in this experience a joy deeper than all the passing joys and sorrows of this life. For Saint Paul, faith is an ongoing, intimate communion with the risen Lord. "By faith we profess our belief in Jesus as our risen Lord...and enter into his death and resurrection through baptism...."[3]

Subsequent Christian thinkers deepened our understanding of faith, often emphasizing faith as either intellectual content or faith as saving, life-changing trust in Christ. Saint Augustine of Hippo (354–430) emphasized faith as a new way to see beyond appearances into the center of all things where God dwells. Saint Thomas Aquinas (c. 1225–1274) zeroed in on faith as God's gift of loving intimacy with him even in this life. Later thinkers developed these two perspectives in various ways, but the two main emphases—faith as knowledge and faith as personal trust—remained constant, one perspective highlighting one, another perspective highlighting the other.

For Catholics, there is nothing "unreasonable" about faith. Faith does not contradict reason but fulfills it. Reason can find evidence for the existence of God, for example, but beyond that faith—that is, personal intimacy with God—is necessary if we would have further knowledge of God.

Note that for Catholics, faith is in God in the Church. We do not identify God with the Church or any aspect of the Church. Rather, God speaks to us *through* the Church—meaning the People of God, not just the hierarchy. But God is bigger than the Church. Indeed, for Catholics, authentic, if incomplete, "Christian faith exists in all Christian communities, not just in the Catholic Church."[4]

Among other things, this means that Catholicism leaves conscience free to find its own way while seeking light from the Church. Faith does not mean that we allow "the teachings of the Church," for example, to replace conscience. In fact, divergence between individual conscience and Church teachings is perfectly possible, and responsible dissent from official Church teachings, in good conscience, always remains a possible option. Some words of G. K. Chesterton, an early twentieth-century convert to Catholicism, are relevant: "Catholics know the two or three transcendental truths on which they do agree; and take rather a pleasure in disagreeing on everything else."

Since the Second Vatican Council in the mid 1960s, Catholic thinkers have developed an appreciation for the communal context of faith, insisting that we live our faith in Christ only as members of the believing community. This perspective insists that faith comes by experiencing the faith of others and by participating in the life of a local faith community. Contemporary social conditions, where alienation and isolation from others is common, no doubt have much to do with the prominence of this perspective on the Church.

Still, it is good to be cautious. Sometimes "community" can be a way to escape our radical solitude before God; it can, in fact, be a way to sidestep experiences necessary for growth in a faith that measures itself not by the opinions and expectations of others but only by the measure of the gospel itself. For all its advantages, for all the ways "community" is a necessary context for and expression of faith, it is important to maintain the life-giving value of prayerful solitude. A faith that cannot be alone, that cannot survive without being constantly "massaged" by communal interaction, may never be more than a superficial faith.

Father Henri Nouwen (1932–1996), one of the most popular spiritual writers of our time, insisted that solitude is absolutely necessary to the life of faith.

> Without solitude it is virtually impossible to live a spiritual life. Solitude begins with a time and place for God, and him alone. If we really believe not only that God exists but also that he is actively present in our lives—healing, teaching, and guiding—we need to set aside a time and space to give him our undivided attention.[5]

At the same time, Father Nouwen also insisted on the necessity of what he called "the discipline of community." What Nouwen meant by "community," however, is far from being anything superficial, far from being a gathering of people seeking escape or refuge.

> Community as discipline is the effort to create a free and empty space among people where together we can practice true obedience. Through the discipline of community we prevent ourselves from clinging to each other in fear and loneliness, and clear free space to listen to the liberating voice of God.[6]

If one of the main reasons people of faith gather is to "cling to each other in fear and loneliness," then we have something that is far from being a community of faith. It may be some other kind of gathering, but it is not a community of faith.

Authentic faith finds itself in both solitude and community; both are necessary to faith, and the two are related to each other. Faith requires that we be able to be alone with God, for only when we can find God in solitude can we find God in community. At the same time, when we find God in community, we will be able to find God in solitude. According to Nouwen:

> When we have come to know the life-giving Spirit of God in the center of our solitude and have thus been able to affirm our true identity, we can also see that same life-giving Spirit speaking to us through our fellow human beings. And when we have come to recognize the life-giving Spirit of God as the source of our life together, we too will more readily hear his voice in our solitude.[7]

The "community" required by authentic faith is not a mere matter of "hanging out" with other people in a churchy, after-Mass, coffee-and-donuts context. It is a much deeper reality. Father Nouwen said that "community does not necessarily mean being physically together. ...The space for God in community transcends all limits of time and place."[8]

Consider a remark made by Flannery O'Connor, one of the great writers of fiction of the twentieth century and a Catholic right down to her toes:

I went to St. Mary's as it was right around the
corner and I could get there practically every morning. I went there three years and never knew a
soul in that congregation or any of the priests,
but it was not necessary. As soon as I went in the
door I was home.[9]

What Flannery O'Connor said is true, but it is questionable whether she could get away with saying it in
today's Church. The "community" that faith gives birth
to, and in which faith is nourished and expresses itself, is
a much deeper reality than the Protestant notion of "fellowship," which is what "community" sometimes seems
to become in Catholic parishes. A parish where a great
deal of yukking-it-up, glad-handing, and coffee-and-
doughnuts groupiness goes on, sometimes even during
the liturgy, is not necessarily a parish that shares a deep
faith, a deep sense of the presence of Christ in its midst.
If we don't understand Flannery O'Connor's experience
of feeling at home in a parish church where she was anonymous, then our understanding of the relationship between
faith and community remains superficial.

Faith—Lived and Real

Because the value of theological theories of faith is limited, let's allow them to slip into the shadows for now.
They are necessary; they are valuable. But for now, let
them slip away. Instead, let's attend to faith as we see it
lived and have seen it lived by real people in the real world.
That is where faith becomes itself, not a theory but a life;
that is where faith takes on flesh.

Think. Remember someone from your past—father,
mother, grandmother, grandfather, uncle, aunt, cousin,

neighbor, friend. Right there in the flesh—in the mostly small, sometimes big ways he or she lived life, right before your curious eyes—years, perhaps many years ago—is the meaning of faith. There is the faith that can fill your own heart with faith and spark your own dedication to living in faith.

Who is the person you think of first? That person may have been no living saint, more likely a fairly average person. If the people who come to mind for me knew that I think of them when I think of faith, they would laugh right out loud. For they never, I swear, thought of themselves as models of faith, paradigms of piety, or ideals from whom anyone else should gather inspiration. Hardly. Ah, but that is how our good God works, you know. Ordinary people do not see it in themselves, but the good God lets others see it in them all the same. All the same, I saw the light of faith.

In the priest who was pastor of the little northern Idaho parish where I was baptized, at the ripe old age of ten, I saw the light of faith. I did. I had the good fortune to find myself in a Catholic school at the beginning of my third-grade year, and into the classroom one day came Father Thomas Lafey. Under a head of thick black hair his whole face smiled, from his eyes to his lips to his cheeks, that always had a four o'clock shadow by ten o'clock in the morning.

What did Father Lafey do to spark faith in me? Lord alone knows. I can pinpoint nothing in particular, but I know that he did. Perhaps he did the most important thing anyone can do: he was himself. He did what a priest did, and he clearly enjoyed doing it. Perhaps on some level of my developing awareness I sensed that whatever it was that enabled Father Lafey to be himself was something I wanted, too. And that something, it soon became clear, was faith. I did not think of it as such, but it was the virtue of faith, the strength to be in the world in ongoing, loving intimacy with the triune God: Father, Son, and Holy Spirit. It was that. It was that, for sure.

Oddly enough, when I think of faith I also think of people close to me who did not have much faith. From these people I saw what a life can be like when faith is weak or absent altogether. That helped me to see the importance of faith, to pray for faith, to try to live my faith, to thank God for my faith, and to learn about faith. That helped me want to share my faith with others, because I saw what a difference faith made in my life. That made me want my own children to embrace their Catholic faith, because I knew that as long as they had this faith their lives would have meaning and purpose, no matter what else they did. Faith would be the "glue" that would hold their lives together. I saw with my own eyes the difference between a life lived in the true light of faith and a life lived in the false light of a culture that cherishes other things.

At the same time, when I think of faith I think of the ways my faith has been nourished by unexpected people— artists, for example, whose faith may not be of the churchgoing variety but whose hearts are with the Divine Mystery and whose work has a radiance that only some kind of faith can be responsible for. I cannot know why such people remain on the sidelines of a full life of faith—God knows—but I can see in their work the light and truth of a genuine, if incomplete, faith.

Singer/songwriter John Stewart, for example, wrote a song called "Botswana," about the helpless anguish of seeing photographs of starving, poverty-stricken children in that much afflicted African nation.[10] In his song, Stewart sings: "Faith it is a fire, and it's fanned by the winds of thanks."

There is much good theology in these words. Absent is the misguided notion, for example, that faith is primarily a condition that requires us to shut down our intellect in order to accept otherwise preposterous propositions—so-called "blind faith." We come across this view of faith when someone says that "you just have to take it on faith." This may reflect an unscientific interpretation of the Bible, for example, or someone may say this as an explanation for why we must accept a religious doctrine. "You just have to take it on faith" means that we should ask no questions and have no doubts. Otherwise we don't "have faith," which means that we are lost. Booga, booga, booga.

Absent, too, in John Stewart's lyrics is the understanding of faith as a "crutch" used by people too weak to stand up and face life on their own two feet. People who are skeptical about religion, particularly "organized religion," sometimes accuse religious people of needing faith as "a crutch." This implies that skepticism, agnosticism, atheism, or simple secular indifference to religion makes them strong and courageous, able to face life head-on with no need for the "crutch" of religious faith.

As John Stewart sings "Botswana," a female backup singer chants over and over, "*Credo Domino*," Latin for "I believe, Lord." Thus do John Stewart's lyrics nourish a balanced understanding of the virtue of faith.

Other artists are Catholics who speak from an ongoing, present experience of faith that they know is the well from which they draw in more ways than one. Ron Hansen, for example, is the author of several novels including *Mariette in Ecstasy* and *Atticus*. Hansen wrote *Mariette in Ecstasy* after studying the writings of Saint Thérèse of Lisieux, the young nineteenth-century Carmelite nun whose simple yet powerful view of faith continues to inspire countless people the world over. The latter novel, *Atticus*, has three levels. On one level, it is something of a murder mystery. On a second level, it is the story of a father-son relationship. On the deepest level, however, *Atticus* is a retelling of the story of the Prodigal Son in the Gospel of Luke.

Ron Hansen's fiction presents faith as a part of the fabric of life, not as something tacked or pasted onto life to refer to only at particular times, like Sundays or holidays or times of crisis. At the same time, Hansen's writing acknowledges that we live in a world where we cannot take for granted that even educated people are familiar with religious texts such as the Gospel of Luke. Thus, in *Atticus,* Hansen summarizes the story of the Prodigal Son at a point in his novel when anyone with even a passing familiarity of the New Testament will know that this is the story to which the novel refers.

For writers and other artists, such as Ron Hansen, faith is foundational to their life and work, yet they know their audience is made up of many people for whom "faith" is an all but meaningless concept. So Hansen writes to express his own faith and, who knows, perhaps some of his readers will find in his words the spark of a new faith for themselves. At the very least, some readers may perceive that faith may not be the intellectually or ethically dishonest "crutch," "escape clause," or "security blanket" they previously thought it was.

Faith is more of a "leap to make" than a "crutch to cling to"; more of a "push to take risks" than an "escape"; a "source of insecurity" rather than "security." Flannery O'Connor once remarked in a letter:

What people don't realize is what religion costs.
They think faith is a big electric blanket, when of
course it is the cross. It is much harder to believe
than not to believe....Don't expect faith to clear
things up for you. It is trust, not certainty.[11]

Faith is not a way out; rather, faith is a way in. In
fact, there are times when authentic Christian faith is the
best way in the world to get yourself into trouble. Faith
is no spiritual aspirin to cure life's headaches. If anything,
we will have more headaches with faith than without it.
At the same time, of course, we will also have more deep-
down, genuine joy. And this is no superficial joy, but the
kind of joy that could, for example, leave Saint Maximilian Kolbe with a smile on his lips as he died in a Nazi
concentration camp during World War II.[12]

Sometimes people think of faith as the source of absolute security. On the contrary, authentic faith is a source
of security only in the way that the love in a good marriage is a source of security, or the affection of two friends
is a source of security. We never know where that marriage or that friendship may take us. In this sense, faith is
best described as an adventure. It might also be seen as a
paradox; it comforts the afflicted *and* afflicts the comfortable.

One of the most lively and creative Christian thinkers of our time is Frederick Buechner, author of numerous novels and works of nonfiction. In his contemporary
classic, *Wishful Thinking*, Buechner wrote that if some-
body had walked up to Jesus as he hung on the cross and
asked him if it hurt, Jesus might well have replied, "Only
when I laugh." "Faith dies, as it lives, laughing." Buechner
also wrote:

Faith is better understood as a verb than as a noun, as a process than as a possession. It is on-again, off-again rather than once-and-for-all. Faith is not being sure where you're going but going anyway. A journey without maps. [Theologian Paul] Tillich said that doubt isn't the opposite of faith; it is an element of faith....I can't prove the friendship of my friend. When I experience it, I don't need to prove it. When I don't experience it, no proof will do. If I tried to put his friendship to the test somehow, the test itself would [ruin] the friendship I was testing. So it is with the Godness of God. ...Almost nothing that makes any real difference can be proved....I cannot prove that life is better than death or love better than hate. I cannot prove the greatness of the great or the beauty of the beautiful....Faith can't prove a damned thing. Or a blessed thing either.[13]

FAITH IS LOVING INTIMACY

It is good to compare faith to a friendship or, even better, to a marriage, because faith at its most basic is intimacy between Godness and humanness. Faith at its most basic is loving intimacy between people and the Creator of the universe, and the Creator is wildly, madly, crazy, in love with each one of us. This relationship exists, take note, not in isolation; it's not a matter of you and God off in a corner by yourselves. As we noted above, faith happens in the context of a community of faith.

The point is not to reduce faith to an experience of "togetherness." Much less should we make faith dependent on a religious version of the modern "herd mentality." Rather, faith comes to us and is lived by us in the context of what the Nicene Creed calls "the communion of saints." We participate in the life of a universal community, one that exists on this earth, in time and space, as well as in eternity. Thus faith draws its life from a universal community's experience of loving intimacy with the risen Christ. If this means, for the individual believer, participation in the life of a local faith community that is characterized by extensive social interaction, this is incidental. It's nice if it happens, but it is not essential if it does not.

At the same time, genuine faith requires a deep awareness that God cannot be separated from other people. Words from the First Letter of John make the point perfectly:

> Those who say, "I love God," and hate their brothers or sisters, are liars; for those who do not love a brother or sister whom they have seen, cannot love God whom they have not seen (4:20).

Faith requires that we live not for ourselves but for others. Authentic Christian faith requires that we live for others, and receiving a reward in return—emotional, psychological, or material—is irrelevant. Placing too great an emphasis on "community" in the life of faith leaves us thinking that if we don't get emotional "payback" for participation in the local community, then faith isn't all it's cracked up to be. "We truly live our faith only in and with and through the believers who are the Church, the community of the 'faithful.'"[14] Nevertheless, the primary purpose of the local faith community is not to provide each person with a warm womb of refuge from the world, but to constitute a community of worship and service.

If anything, the Jesus of the gospels downplays the

value of relationships with people we like and enjoy being with, while highlighting the importance of relationships with those for whom we do not have a natural affection:

> "If you do good to those who do good to you, what credit is that to you? For even sinners do the same. If you lend to those from whom you hope to receive, what credit is that to you? Even sinners lend to sinners, to receive as much again. But love your enemies, do good, and lend, expecting nothing in return" (Luke 6:33–35a).

The relationships that are most important to faith are not the relationships referred to by the Protestant notion of "fellowship." Rather, the relationships that are crucial in the life of faith are those between believers and those that faith calls them to care for. Jesus does not say that the eternal destiny of his followers depended on whether or not they "built community." Rather, in Matthew's Gospel, in the story of the sheep and the goats, we learn that what matters most is our dedication to serving the real needs of others, whether we find them to be jolly companions or not. "Truly I tell you, just as you did it to one of the least of these who are members of my family, you did it to me" (25:40).

Faith is rooted in the loving intimacy of the faith community, and the loving intimacy of the individual with God, who is love. Indeed, faith *is* this loving intimacy. At the same time, this relationship we call faith leads to knowledge and understanding—like the kind of knowledge and understanding that comes from any personal relationship. In other words, faith gives rise to a desire to better understand the Divine Mystery, the God we know and love through faith.

Conclusion

Just as two people who sense the beginnings of friendship naturally want to know more about each other, faith often expresses itself through a desire for knowledge and understanding. A mature faith, the faith of a grown-up, is a faith that grows by learning—by reading books on religious topics, sound theology, and spirituality, and by participation in study and discussion groups. A mature faith is a faith that will not settle for an understanding of one's religion carried over from childhood or adolescence.

Faith is never "blind." Rather, faith is a way to see with the heart as well as with the mind. Faith brings heart and intellect into harmony with each other. "Ultimately," wrote Thomas Merton, "faith is the only key to the universe. The final meaning of human existence, and the answers to the questions on which all our happiness depends cannot be found in any other way."[15]

Chapter Two

§

THE VIRTUE
OF HOPE

Singer/songwriter John Stewart included the following lyrics in one of his songs: "Hope is like despair, it won't get you anywhere." These lyrics seem to represent hope as mere wishing, and as ineffectual as despair, which many people see as an opposite to hope.

The important thing is to understand what hope is—and what it is not. Hope is not the same thing as saying, "I wish this or that would happen." The virtue of hope is much deeper than that. In fact, the virtue of hope is called "theological," because it directs us toward personal union with God, to a far more significant place than that occupied by mere optimism.

AUTHENTIC HOPE

The theological virtue of hope is central to the entire Bible. No matter which biblical book we open, we find encouragement to a life based on authentic hope. The story of Moses and the Exodus, for example, is a story designed to inspire hope. Through long years of slavery in Egypt, the people of Israel did not give up hope that they would be liberated. During the years of wandering in the desert, they did not give up hope. Even when they did lapse briefly, by building themselves a golden calf and worshiping it, God did not give up on them.

In the gospels, Jesus' most basic message is one of hope. He declares that the kingdom, or reign, of God is at hand. The power of Jesus' own Resurrection is present and active in the lives of his people here and now, so there is no need for anything but hope in a destiny that is assured by the death and Resurrection of Jesus. Authentic Christian hope is exemplified in the words T. S. Eliot places on the lips of Saint Thomas Becket, in Eliot's play, *Murder in the Cathedral*. Becket says, "I am not in danger: only near to death."[1]

Saint Paul waxes eloquent when he talks about hope, describing hope as the dynamic reality at the heart of all creation:

> We know that the whole creation has been groaning in labor pains until now; and not only the creation, but we ourselves, who have the first fruits of the Spirit, groan inwardly while we wait for adoption, the redemption of our bodies. For in hope we were saved. Now hope that is seen is not hope. For who hopes for what is seen? But if we hope for what we do not see, we wait for it with patience (Romans 8:22–25).

We can look for—and find—hope and the true meaning of hope in the lives of the people in our world. Paul Tomasik, a Catholic high-school student, found a deep source of hope in the life of his grandfather, Arthur J.

Hallinan.[2] Following his grandfather's death just shy of age eighty, Paul discovered all the good his grandfather had done in quiet, unspectacular ways. For example, Arthur Hallinan kept a spiritual journal for many years. He had his own prayer book, put together from prayers he typed himself. He also donated money each month to various charities; learned New Testament Greek so he could work out his own translations of scriptural passages from the original texts; taught himself Braille so he could be a volunteer for the Society of the Blind; and supported one of his nephews as a conscientious objector during the Vietnam War, even though as a World War II veteran he disagreed.

"I am beginning to realize only now," Paul wrote, "that his values, his spirituality, and his ministry have left me a legacy of hope and inspiration for the future."[3]

Hope is the virtue that enables us to live for the future without knowing what that future may bring. While optimism believes that nothing but good is just around the corner, hope, on the other hand, believes that life is worth living *whatever* is just around the corner or not. G. K. Chesterton explained hope well: "As long as matters are really hopeful, hope is a mere flattery or platitude; it is only when everything is hopeless that hope begins to be a strength at all."[4]

Hope is just as possible in apparently hopeless circumstances as it is anyplace else. Hope has an infinitely larger perspective than does mere optimism. Hope's perspective is eternal, whereas optimism is limited to the here-and-now. Hope comes to life when the night is darkest, long after optimism has given up the ghost.

The life-giving power of hope shows itself most forcefully in the face of risk and suffering. One of the most dramatic examples of hope is found in the life of Saint

Thomas More (1478–1545). Because More refused to support King Henry VIII's divorce and decision to establish the Church of England (Anglican) in opposition to the Roman Catholic Church, More was condemned to death. Henry had Thomas More imprisoned in the Tower of England for fifteen months, then ordered his execution.

Throughout his ordeal, Thomas More remained firm in his faith, with no wish to die or become a martyr. All the same, because he had the virtue of hope, Thomas More was able to think in terms larger than the present moment or even the present era. He was able to keep his values in order. At the last moment, as the executioner readied him to die, Thomas made his priorities clear. "I die the king's good servant," he said, "but God's first."[5]

Hope also makes it possible for us to remain faithful to our covenant promises, marriage being one of the best examples of a covenant promise based on the virtue of hope. The vows of marriage, for example, express the covenant promise of a man and a woman to remain faithful to each other "as long as we both shall live." The virtue of hope makes it possible for husband and wife to see beyond the present moment, to think of their marriage in the larger context of their entire lives, and even to ponder eternity. Hope makes it possible to keep in perspective the difficulties, anguish, or outright suffering the present may bring. When we're in the midst of a difficult—perhaps even impossible—situation, hope whispers a reminder to us: "This too shall pass."

To borrow images from other John Stewart lyrics, hope makes it possible to see that even the darkest of times are but "the shadows of the angels wings."[6] Hope knows that "when things go wrong, they happen for the best." Simple, even simple-minded, as this idea may sound, in the real circumstances of our real lives, there is nothing simple about it. Hope can mean the difference between life and death; it can be the only alternative to utter despair.

Authentic hope is all the more remarkable because its source rests in sheer trust in God's word and promise, not in tangible evidence. Saint Paul makes this point in the Letter to the Romans, while at the same time making clear the connection between hope and faith:

> Hoping against hope, [Abraham] believed that he would become "the father of many nations," according to what was said, "So numerous shall your descendants be." He did not weaken in faith when he considered his own body, which was already as good as dead (for he was about a hundred years old), or when he considered the barrenness of Sarah's womb (4:18–19).

Hope, in other words, is most authentic when there seems to be no basis for it. Hope does not draw its life from visible signs that indicate "things may be looking up." Rather, hope gets a grip based on faith—the heart's conviction that God is trustworthy even when there is no earthly evidence to support such a claim.

Paul uses Abraham as an example of hope, because Abraham did not give mere lip service to God's trustworthiness; Abraham actually took action based on that trust. Abraham lived by hope even when doing so required him to accept suffering and sacrifice.

Ultimately, "Christian hope is grounded...in the loving generosity of God, manifested to us constantly and most particularly in the sacrificial death of Christ."[7] In other words, the ultimate "evidence" upon which hope is based is faith that God's love in Christ is worth our trust here and now, in our own life and in the lives of those we care for.

The virtue of hope is genuine when it refuses to cling to any particular outcome. Hope does not expect anything in particular; it does not dictate to God a specific result. Hope does not say, "Here is what I hope for, and if I don't get it, then nuts on you, God." Rather, hope says, "Here is the situation, and I leave it in your hands, God. Do what you will, because only you know what is best for all concerned."

HOPE—LIVED AND REAL

Most of us do not live in abstract terms, of course. Our lack of hope usually expresses itself in concrete and perhaps mundane ways. We hope, to be sure, but our hope is not in God's love. Rather, we believe that hope is most likely to be fulfilled by money and financial game-playing—not by God. Hope will be fulfilled, we believe, by certificates of deposit, insurance policies, investments, stocks and bonds, mutual funds. These, ah yes, these are what we hope for, because these we can expect to fulfill our hopes for this life. We would like nothing more than to win a few million dollars in a state lottery. In fact, we "hope" that we will one day win precisely such a treasure. Yet to "hope" for such an occurrence is a perversion of the true virtue of hope. For hope is only true when it has no expectations, when it opens the heart wide to whatever may happen in the providence of God, believing that whatever God's providence yields is, indeed, good. To "hope" to win millions in the lottery is to miss completely the spiritual dangers inherent in such an event.

A most excellent example of how a misguided sense

of hope might rescue itself in such circumstances actually happened in November 1997. Seventy-three-year-old Eleanor Boyer of Immaculate Conception Parish in Somerville, New Jersey, won over eight million dollars in the state lottery. Immediately, Eleanor Boyer announced that she would give away every penny to various charities. "I have my pension and Social Security," she said. "Why let the money sit in the bank till I die?"[8]

Three weeks after she hit the jackpot that countless people would have given almost anything to get, Eleanor Boyer gave over five million dollars to her parish of twenty-eight hundred families, which includes an elementary school and a high school. The rest she gave to various "good causes," to needy individuals in her neighborhood, and to her three nephews, her only close relatives.

Eleanor Boyer did not allow winning millions of greenbacks to change her life even slightly. She did not buy a new car, but kept on driving her faded, yellow, twenty-eight-year-old Chevy Malibu. She continued wearing the same sensible shoes, and she did not buy herself a big new house, preferring the little gray house where she was born in 1924. Eleanor went on attending daily Mass and spending time with her friends and neighbors, as she always did. Her life was not changed by winning millions of clams. She felt relieved, in fact, when she finally managed to give away all the money. It was a burden she was happy to be rid of.

Is buying lottery tickets contrary to the virtue of hope? Once again, Eleanor Boyer stands as a fine example. She always said that if she won she would give half of her winnings to the Church. But she never expected to win— a realistic expectation given the odds—and she never prayed to win. In fact, she often failed to check to see if she had won. She always said that when she bought a

lottery ticket she viewed it as a simple two-dollar dona-
tion to the state education fund, which is where all ex-
cess New Jersey lottery funds go.

Christian faith offers no easy answers, not even to
the question of buying lottery tickets and what to do with
the money if you win. Each person's situation is unique.
But Eleanor Boyer of Somerville, New Jersey, offers an
excellent example of what the virtue of hope is likely to
do with unexpected wealth—of what Jesus would do in
similar circumstances.

A contemporary writer describes the virtue of hope
as "an unflinching, bold, and persistent capacity in the
present moment to seize a future that is possible yet un-
seen."[9] This description contradicts the common assumption that hope is the refuge of the spiritual weakling, the
final refuge of those not courageous enough to fling themselves back into the fray following failure or discourage-
ment. On the contrary, hope is "unflinching, bold, and persistent." The virtue of hope is so firmly convinced that the
present can be improved upon, that it slogs through even
great catastrophes in order to build a better tomorrow.

Mind you, hope is not presumption. Presumption gets
a load of what the present moment has to offer, and then
turns and runs in the other direction, calling over its shoulder, "You take care of it, God!" Hope, on the other hand,
resolutely faces the real situation at hand, disastrous as it
may be, and relies on God's grace to pick up the pieces,
rebuild, and move on.

One of the great spiritual masters of our era was Thomas Merton, Trappist monk, author, and poet (1917–
1968). Merton wrote:

We are not perfectly free until we live in pure hope. For when our hope is pure, it no longer trusts exclusively in human and visible means, nor rests in any visible end. He who hopes in God trusts God, whom he never sees, to bring him to the possession of things that are beyond imagination.[10]

In other words, hope is not hope as long as it has a specific outcome in mind. Therefore, hope requires us to be free people, liberated from dependence on anything but God.

On a personal level, hope urges us to be free from addictions. Because everyone has addictions, this observation is not just about those with addictions to alcohol, nicotine, or other drugs. Gerald G. May, M.D., wrote:

I am not being flippant when I say that all of us suffer from addiction....I mean in all truth that the psychological, neurological, and spiritual dynamics of full-fledged addiction are actively at work within every human being.[11]

In traditional spiritual terms, we might substitute "attachment" for "addiction." We become "attached" to all kinds of things, from food to sexual pleasure to the opinions of others to a particular lifestyle. These things hold us in chains, and the larger part of each of us is unwilling to let go, even to be genuinely free. Only the grace of God—another name for God's gift of himself to human persons—is more powerful than attachments or addictions. According to May:

Grace is the most powerful force in the universe. It can transcend repression, addiction, and every other internal or external power that seeks to oppress the freedom of the human heart. Grace is where our hope lies.[12]

Let us not think of grace, however, as a *deus ex machina*, a magic fix that will come flying out of nowhere. Here is what we mean by the kind of grace that hope relies upon. On a visit to Guatemala, I traveled the Pan-American Highway—nothing grand, just a two-lane paved road constantly in need of repairs—to the high mountains where the Quiché Indian people live. These people are poor, often living in primitive circumstances with little medical care.

One day we climbed a high hill, through acres of corn, to the home of an old woman. This woman lived in a hut made of dried corn stalks lashed together, with a hard dirt floor, and an open fire pit in the middle for heat and cooking. The old woman's eyes were red with infections caused by the smoke from her fire, and her situation seemed hopeless. I wondered how she could have survived such a life for so many years. Yet in her beaming face I saw Something More. This was a woman filled with a hope that had no discernible basis, and because I saw God's love in her face, I, too, felt myself becoming more hopeful.

HOPE PLACES ALL IN GOD'S HANDS

Hope draws its life from a faith that is in touch with God's love, a faith that knows things will change, perhaps dramatically, in God's own good time. Therefore, hope stays put, faces reality, and works to improve the situation, without expecting a magical reversal of negative conditions as a result of those efforts. Hope waits patiently and works patiently, knowing that, when the time is right, the walls will come down, the chains will be loosed, and the prison doors will swing open.

Only authentic hope, for example, can make it possible for someone to work patiently to alleviate unjust social conditions. Someone dedicated to helping people in oppressed economic conditions will survive only on the virtue of hope, which depends on a deep religious faith. The person who is a mere social activist, who embraces the lot of the poor and works tirelessly to overcome the causes of poverty, but has no authentic hope, will sooner or later "burn out" and give up in despair. Such persons, in fact, have been known to commit suicide. The cause of such a death can be attributed to depression, yes, but also to a lack of the virtue of hope. These people make the mistake of thinking that they themselves must bring about the changes that will alleviate poverty and injustice. When a person acts on this assumption, and conditions do not change, despair is a virtual certainty. The virtue of hope, on the other hand, continues to act day after day, week after week, month after month, year after year, placing all in the hands of God. People of hope act as if all depends on them—but pray as if all depends on God. People of hope may wonder why God does not bring about change immediately, but they are able to live with the mystery, the not knowing.

Hope is evident in the life of Dorothy Day (1897–1980), cofounder of the Catholic Worker Movement. Dorothy Day opposed injustice and poverty her entire adult life, but she had no illusions about being able to bring about a new social and economic order through her own efforts. Because she was strong in the virtue of hope, Day was able to carry out the works of mercy, day after day, for many years, doing what she could to meet people's immediate needs for food and clothing. After ten, twenty, thirty, and forty years of participating in nonviolent demonstrations to oppose policies that led to poverty, injustice, and war, Day saw that poverty, injustice, and war were just as evident as when she first began. Yet she did not despair. Because she cultivated the virtue of hope, Day did not give up. She understood, in her deepest center, that everything did not depend on her. She understood that once she had done all she could do, once she had done her best, she could leave everything to God. She could "let go and let God." This is how hope shows itself, in the knowledge that we can do only so much to change things, and after that, it is up to God, in his own good time, to bring about change in ways that no human effort will ever accomplish. This may happen in our lifetime, or it may not.

One of the best examples of this is the sudden crumbling of international Communism in the late 1980s. Imagine asking people just two years—even one year—prior to the destruction of the Berlin Wall, which divided East Germany from West Germany, if that would ever happen. Invariably the answer would have been, "No," or "Not in my lifetime." The Berlin Wall had been a fact of life for almost forty years, a symbol of a divided Germany that seemed permanent. When East Germany's hard-line Communist government was forced from power in September 1989, and the wall suddenly came down on November 9, 1989, the world was overwhelmed with astonishment. It was as if the removal of the wall had "just happened." It came "out of the blue," with no advance notice.

This is the kind of event that hope believes in. Without knowing how or when it will happen, hope believes such a thing will, in fact, happen. Metaphorically speaking, it's almost as if the situation is locked into place, then suddenly, somewhere, a cosmic key turns in the lock, certain cosmic tumblers fall into place, a cosmic door swings open, and everything is different. Hope does all it can to bring truth and light, grace and peace, into a given situation, knowing that the most its efforts can do is bring some relief.

The question we face on an everyday basis, however, is the question of how to cultivate hope in the ordinary, knockabout world, in our ordinary day-in, day-out lives. We want to be hope-filled people, but we find ourselves constantly needing to resist the double temptations of presumption, on the one hand, and despair on the other. How can we nourish authentic hope without being presumptuous? How can we be hopeful without being merely optimistic, which can easily lead to despair?

Listen. Hope does not come from a constant, gargantuan act of the will, some kind of inner straining to "be hopeful." Hope does not come from pretending that there is no darkness, suffering, injustice, poverty, pain, or ordinary daily anguish. Being hopeful does not mean putting on an act: "Here I am, a regular little sunbeam. Nothing can make me feel blue." Hope does not come from a daily effort to "walk on the sunny side of the street."

No. Listen. Here is perhaps a surprise. There is something unnatural about hope! Hope is not our natural condition. Take a look around, take a quick 360-degree look around. Despair is easy to find on all sides. Influences of all kinds, here and there, militate against being hopeful. Take a look at the high suicide rate, the large percentage of people who think euthanasia and abortion are civilized ideas, the prevalence of drug abuse, the violence in our streets, the high demand for psychiatric care, the general listlessness among many young people. Get an earful of the lyrics in much of the popular music. One of the few places we are likely to find support for genuine hope is among religious people who have their act together.

Listen. Hope is not nourished by a society that encourages us to be self-centered and selfish as a way of life. Hope is not nourished by a culture that tells us to have confidence in the attainment of an increasingly affluent lifestyle as the only way to be truly happy. Hope is not nourished by a world that cultivates individualism and tells us that the only thing we can believe in and count on is ourselves.

The virtue of hope survives and thrives when we know from experience that life is worth living only when we serve and care for others. The virtue of hope survives and thrives when we know from firsthand experience that happiness happens when we forget self to love and care for others. The virtue of hope fills the human heart when we learn from personal experience what it is to love God for his own sake.

One of the most popular mistakes people make today, one that drives hope from the human heart, is the *faith* people have in this idea: that sex separated from commitment is a balanced, healthy idea. This belief, far from liberating, reflects both despair and presumption. The belief that sex separated from commitment is a morally neutral choice reflects despair over the possibility of authentic, deep human intimacy. It says that shared sexual pleasure has no necessary connection to a prior permanent commitment in marriage.

This belief embodies presumption, because it presumes that sex separated from marriage will have no negative consequences on society at large and no negative consequences on relationships with other individuals in the present or the future. Just the opposite is true, of course. For starters, major studies show that the divorce rate nearly doubles among couples who cohabit prior to marriage, yet this practice has gained widespread social acceptance—a sign not of hope but of despair.[13]

CONCLUSION

The virtue of hope, or the lack of the virtue of hope, reveals itself in our attitudes toward life and the world, and in our relationships with other people. Ultimately hope is rooted in our relationship with God and our openness to God's love. To love God is to have hope that God will be there if we trust that he loves and cares for us beyond the boundaries of the present moment—even beyond the limits of time and space. "Better than hoping for anything from the Lord, besides His love, let us place all our hope in His love itself. This hope is as sure as God Himself."[14]

Chapter Three

❧

THE VIRTUE
OF LOVE

P eople of a certain age recall the time in the late
1960s when the world's most popular rock
group, the Beatles, sang, "All you need is love,
love...love is all you need." The authors of the song, John
Lennon and Paul McCartney, were astonishingly naive.
At the time, they actually seemed to have thought that all
they needed to do was point out to the world the importance of love, sing about it, and the world would overcome its many woes in no time. At the same time, Lennon
and McCartney were perfectly correct, for if we understand
the meaning of "love" that is precisely "all you need."

AUTHENTIC LOVE

Italian poet Dante Alighieri (1265–1321), best known
for *The Divine Comedy,* might well agree with the Beatles.
"Love is the heartbeat of the whole universe," he wrote.
"Everything participates in it according to its own special love, from simple bodies, to composite bodies, to
plants, to animals, to man."[1]

The Christian virtue of authentic love is not romantic love—although there is certainly a place for romantic love. The Christian understanding of the virtue of love may be clarified if we trace the term to its Greek and Latin origins. The Greek word for love is *agape*. In Latin, *love* derives from *caritas*, from which we get the English word, *charity*. In both cases, the meaning of *love* is "an affective disposition toward another person arising from qualities perceived as attractive, from instincts of natural relationship, or from sympathy, and resulting in concern for the welfare of the object and usually also delight in her/his/its presence and desire for the beloved's acceptance and approval."[2]

If we look at love from a theological point of view, it is usually understood to be God's unconditional, benevolent love.[3] By extension, we need to discuss God's love for us, our love for God, our love for one another, our love for God's creation, and a properly understood love for our own self. It should be clear by now that "love" is far from being a simple topic! All the same, the virtue of love is absolutely basic to a Christian life, so we do well to give it our full attention.

God's love is behind and supports all other loves. Indeed, before we can love well we need to consciously open ourselves to God's love so that love can have a healing effect on us from the inside out. Sometimes it is important during young adulthood, before any permanent life commitments are made, to make room for what we might call the "prayer of contemplative love."

Now there is nothing esoteric about this kind of prayer. To practice the prayer of contemplative love simply means to make time in each day—ten or fifteen minutes is a good starting point—to open ourselves to God's love. Although this may include allowing the word of

God to sink into our heart and live there through the slow, meditative reading of Scripture, it must include some time of sitting or kneeling quietly, simply being open to God's love. Focus may be maintained by slowly repeating a short prayer or line from Scripture. "My God and my all." "Oh God, you are my God whom I seek." "Love of God, fill my heart." Those who practice the prayer of contemplative love on a daily basis, even for just a few weeks, will discover a new, more alive capacity to love and be loved.

God is love's starting point. Throughout the Hebrew Scriptures, or Old Testament, God appears as the faithful lover of his people, and the relationship between God and the individual person is described in terms of loving intimacy. The Septuagint, the pre-Christian Greek translation of the Hebrew Scriptures, uses the word *agapao* primarily to refer to human relationships, especially sexual attraction between men and women. At the same time, the Septuagint applies this word to the love of family and friends, and to describe the basis of family and community life. In all of these uses, however, the word *agapao* has a clearly practical character: one *acts* on behalf of the one who is loved.[4] Love is not merely an emotion, thought, or intention. Something *happens*.

In order for the virtue of love to be authentic it must be active in ways that help the one loved to *feel* loved. You can tell me thirty times a day that you love me, but unless you act in ways that leave me *feeling* loved and *knowing* that I am loved, your love is a pure abstraction as far as I'm concerned, only words. This means, for example, that in order for a husband to feel loved, his wife must express her love in ways that feel like love to him. It's important for husband and wife to say "I love you" to each other, but it is also important for a husband to bring his wife flowers, take responsibility for his share of the household chores and parenting duties, and do his best to be the kind of lover his wife prefers. The loving wife reciprocates, of course, by bringing unexpected gifts that suit her husband's interests, by carrying her share of the financial duties, and by doing her best to be the kind of lover her husband appreciates. It is important for the two of them to discover what love "feels like" to the other, and to respond accordingly. Perhaps she feels loved when he suggests that she take an evening away from home by herself to do whatever she enjoys doing. Perhaps he feels loved when she gives him a book by his favorite author. The point is that when two people genuinely love each other, love shows itself when the one loved feels loved.

The high point of the Old Testament's understanding of the unity between human and divine love occurs in the Song of Songs, a celebration of passionate sexual love. So true is this that blushing translators sometimes feel obliged to tone down what the Hebrew text actually says. One scholarly translator offers examples from the original Hebrew text that we usually do not find in English translations. Note that the first section is from a male perspective, the second from a female perspective:[5]

> A garden locked is my sister bride, / A pool locked, a fountain sealed. / Your groove a pomegranate grove / With fruits delectable (4:12–13)....
>
> My love thrust his "hand" [Hebrew euphemism][6] into the hole, / And my inwards seethed for him (5:4).

The theological virtue of love should not be limited to the realm of the purely spiritual, however, because human love, whether for God or for other people, can never be a purely spiritual. Especially in the sacrament of marriage, the unity of spiritual and physical love deserves to be taken seriously. After all, we are not pure spirits but *embodied* spirits.

Other sections of the Hebrew Scriptures also use marital imagery to illustrate God's love. The prophets, for example, describe God as a passionate, unfailing, always faithful lover, the one who will not leave even when his people are unfaithful or reject him. Note this passage from Isaiah:

> For your Maker is your husband,
>   the LORD of hosts is his name;...
> For the LORD has called you
>   like a wife forsaken and grieved in spirit,
> like the wife of a man's youth when she is cast off,
>   says your God.
> For a brief moment I abandoned you,
>   but with great compassion I will gather you.
> In overflowing wrath for a moment
>   I hid my face from you,
> but with everlasting love I will have compassion
>   on you,
>   says the LORD, your Redeemer (54:5–8).

In the Hebrew Scriptures, God's love is evident in his always reliable actions on behalf of his people. God leads Israel out of slavery in Egypt, gives them a land flowing with milk and honey, and inspires the Torah. In Deuteronomy, Israel's experience of God's love is the reason to love and obey him in return:

Hear, O Israel: The LORD is our God, the LORD alone. You shall love the LORD your God with all your heart, and with all your soul, and with all your might (6:4–5).

For the ancient Israelites, love was both sensual and affective. The Hebrew Scriptures show us a love that is also a love for neighbor and a love that is faithful to the covenant with God and to the Mosaic Law.

In the New Testament, the model of love is Jesus, of course, and his willingness to give his life for those he loves. Saint Paul, in his famous ode in 1 Corinthians, declares that "faith, hope, and love abide, these three; and the greatest of these is love [*agapē*]" (13:13). His words describe both God's love for us, and the ways in which we are called to love God and others. Not without reason, then, do we think of love as the heart and soul of the Christian life.

All this is abstract, however. These are beautiful ideas that need expression in the real world before we can truly begin to understand the virtue of love. As with all the virtues, we learn best about love when we see it active in the life of a real person, someone who, by his or her life, puts flesh on the principles, abstractions, and ideas.

LOVE—LIVED AND REAL

Saint Thomas Aquinas (thirteenth century), one of the most influential theologians of all time, said that to love is to will the good of the other, which is about as concise a definition as we are likely to find. Aquinas captures the fundamental meaning of love. Notice, however, that he in no way suggests that in order to love we must also "like" the one we love. On the contrary. Christian love, agapē, is dedicated service to the good of the other, and "liking" often has nothing to do with it.

There are many excellent examples of heroic love, of course, even in our own time. Mother Teresa of Calcutta, who gave her life to serving the poorest of the poor, is one of the best known. But as valuable as the example of a Mother Teresa surely is, most people never met her in person; rather, they gathered inspiration from her at a great distance.

For most of us, the greatest teacher of love is probably someone close to us, someone who, day by day, show us the meaning of love. This may be a parent, grandparent, spouse, friend. Indeed, for many people the experience of "falling in love" and, subsequently, "being in love" carries more than a little of God's saving love, and Scripture does not hesitate to capitalize on this human experience to teach us about God's love for us.

Psychologist Erich Fromm essentially built on the insight of Thomas Aquinas when he said in the mid 1950s that love is an action, not a feeling:

Love is the active concern for the life and the growth of that which we love. Where this active concern is lacking, there is no love.[7]

We can learn much from scriptural, historical, and scientific studies of love, to be sure. But we can learn a great deal, too, from the arts—poetry, fiction, music, drama, and so forth. It is the rare mature individual, for example, who reads or hears Shakespeare's Sonnet 116 for the first time without a flash of insight, without believing that he or she now knows something new about love. Read slowly:

Let me not to the marriage of true minds
Admit impediments. Love is not love
Which alters when it alteration finds,
Or bends with the remover to remove.
Oh no! It is an ever-fixèd mark
That looks on tempests and is never shaken,
Whose worth's unknown, although his height
    be taken.
Love's not Time's fool, though rosy lips and cheeks
Within his bending sickle's compass come.
Love alters not with his brief hours and weeks,
But bears it out even to the edge of doom.
    If this be error and upon me proved,
    I never writ, nor no man ever loved.

Shakespeare says what Aquinas and Fromm said, but he says it poetically. Still, even Shakespeare's vision is limited.

Other poets remind us of the meaning of God's love for us. Mark Van Doren (1894–1972) wrote, for example, in his poem "He Loves Me":

That God should love me is more wonderful
Than that I so imperfectly love him.
My reason is mortality, and dim
Senses; his—oh, insupportable—
Is that he sees me. Even when I pull
Dark thoughts about my head, each vein and limb
Delights him.[8]

Van Doren gets to the heart of the matter when it comes to love—for the key to the mystery of love is not a grim determination to love others because it is "the right thing to do," although sometimes this is necessary. Rather, the key to loving is the experience of being loved, and the most important experience in this regard is the experience of being loved by God. Nothing can substitute for the realization that I am loved unconditionally by God, and the only reason God needs to love me "is that he sees me."

In our era, as in many others, of course, there is a pervasive cultural ethos which holds that God, if there is a God, is irrelevant to ordinary human affairs. Religion, institutional or personal, is relegated to the sphere of the private, the personal, something like a hobby we pursue on our own time. God, therefore, is unreal, and the idea of experiencing God's love is quietly preposterous, a notion we find embarrassing. If we have experienced God's love, we should keep it to ourselves, because most people will have not a clue as to what we are talking about.

In such a cultural context, human love becomes the most anyone can hope for, and for countless people this is the only kind of love they ever find, if they find this much. Indeed, for those fortunate enough to have a healthy, loving marriage, the experience of this love opens doors to their inner selves that might otherwise have remained closed forever. So let us give credit where credit is due. In a culture where secular and sacred are alienated from each other, human love can sometimes work near miracles for people. Indeed, Catholicism would insist that in such cases human love becomes a channel for God's love for people who are, at best, religiously indifferent.

For those who manage to cultivate religious faith with some form of integrity, however, God's love is the mystery at the heart of their own, and the world's, existence. Somewhere along the way, they learn by their own experience what Mark Van Doren's poem means and where it came from in his own experience. Even in a culture where holy and profane are so totally divorced from each other, as they are in our culture, a great number of people experience God's love as the ultimate reality.

Once the foundational experience of being loved— by God, by another person, or both—is there to shape our perspective on life and the world, everything will be different. Now the conviction can take shape in our own heart that only love can give life meaning. The only life worth living is a life dedicated in some way to loving others. For most of us, this takes the form of marriage and family life. Marriage and parenting are the most natural and appropriate ways to grow in selflessness and to do the daily work necessary to become an ever more loving person.

A healthy, loving, marriage between a mature man and a mature woman—and relative maturity may be all most of us can hope for—and raising children together constitute the most natural, and so the most holy, way to grow in the virtue of love. The day-after-dayness of being married, the constant challenge and reward of living with another imperfect human being, and the never-a-dull-moment challenges and rewards of parenthood combine to call forth the best and the worst in us. They call for a love that is practical and not dependent on the fleeting feelings of the moment. Although spouses need to work at keeping the romance alive in their marriage, the love that keeps their marriage going is the plain choice to act in a loving manner. Although parents can count on their children to bring them deep joy and satisfaction, there will be many times when raising children is a source of deep anguish. In the former case, love is easy; in the latter case, love is difficult, indeed. But love is just as real in both cases.

In other vocations, too, love is the heart of the matter. Indeed, there is no Christian way of life that is not a life based on the virtue of love. Single people need to shape their lives in ways that help them love. This includes the work or careers they choose, as well as the ways in which they use their free time. This is a particularly crucial issue in a culture that encourages single people to focus on making themselves comfortable and having as much "fun" as possible.

Those called to the ordained priesthood learn that celibacy, too, is for the sake of loving relationships, not for the purpose of distancing oneself from others. To embrace religious celibacy is a way to open oneself to God and neighbor, not a way to close oneself off from personal relationships in order to seek "higher things." Clearly, the virtue of love is just as vital to the life of a priest or a member of a religious order or congregation as it is to anyone else. Although some of the ways priests and religious express their love will be different from the ways married couples and parents express their love, their love will be just as authentic as the love of a noncelibate.

Love Is Shaped by the Words of Jesus

The virtue of love is the glue that holds any life together. If love is not there, everything falls apart. The virtue of love is like the keystone in an arch. If the keystone is not there, the arch collapses. Many people do not understand that Christian faith highlights the unity of love of God and love of neighbor and the vital need for both to be a part of a our existence.

We need to allow God time to show his love for us, and we need to give time to loving God in return. Simply put, if the virtue of love is to be a reality, we need to make time for daily prayer of some kind. Through prayer we come to know God's love, to love God in return, and to love other people faithfully. Grounded in love, we are able to remain faithful to commitments such as marriage, parenthood, priesthood, religious life, or the single life.

The ideal for cultivating the virtue of love is to become devout without being pietistic. This means being sincere and earnest about our faith while avoiding any inclination to be publicly pious in a self-righteous way. Religion gets a bad name from people who constantly fill their talk with pietistic prattle, who surround themselves with religious trinkets, and who indulge in pious devotional practices that border on a belief in magic. The virtue of love is free of all this while, at the same time, having a rock-solid commitment to living a life rooted in lively intimacy with the risen Christ. When the virtue of love is authentically Christian, it acts in union with and carries the spirit of Jesus. This is a love that constantly echoes and is shaped by the words of Jesus in the Gospel of John: "This is my commandment, that you love one another as I have loved you. No one has greater love than this, to lay down one's life for one's friends" (15:12–13).

This is the standard, then: to love as Jesus loved, to "lay down one's life for one's friends." Even more radically, to love as Jesus loved is to enter into an active love for those who are not "one's friends":

> "Love your enemies, do good to those who hate you, bless those who curse you, pray for those who abuse you. If anyone strikes you on the cheek, offer the other also; and from anyone who takes away your coat do not withhold even your shirt" (Luke 6:27–29).

When we hear such words, of course, our inclination is to think literally, to think of extraordinary situations in which we might actually be called upon to love someone who hates us, to give away both coat and shirt. This mind-set, however, fails to understand that the virtue of love is rarely needed in extraordinary situations. Rather, it is in our everyday relationships with family, friends, and coworkers where we find ourselves called upon to both lay down our life for our friends and do good to those whose behavior irritates us.

Think of the most ordinary events of life. The "enemy" we are called to love is the spouse who insists on irritating us by squeezing the toothpaste tube in the middle; the two-year-old who drives us right up the wall; the teenager who shows no respect; the coworker who is the last person in the world we would choose to spend time with. The "friends" we are called to lay down our life for are first of all the members of our family: our spouse, our children, our parents. The virtue of love is not something we live in extraordinary situations; we live it every day.

Most of us intuitively grasp the importance of love; we want to love and we want to be loved. But if we are honest with ourselves, we must admit that what we want most is to be loved. What we fail to see or understand is that our desperate seeking to be loved is the surest way not to be loved. "True happiness is found in unselfish love," Thomas Merton wrote, "a love which increases in proportion as it is shared."[9]

Life has meaning only to the extent that we forget ourselves in order to love others: this is the ultimate lesson of adulthood. But that is not all, for we cannot truly love unless we are willing to accept the love of others in return. "Selfless love consents to be loved selflessly for the sake of the beloved."[10]

To love is to receive love, but we can only receive love by loving. This is the powerful and mysterious paradox of love. While the natural inclination may be to abandon ourselves to ethereal notions of love after reflecting along these lines, we have to keep our feet firmly planted on the ground. The virtue of love is a form of strength, as in the famous words of Dostoevsky's monk, Zossima:

> Active love is a harsh and fearful thing compared with love in dreams. Love in dreams thirsts for immediate action, quickly performed, and with everyone watching. Indeed, it will go as far as the giving even of one's life, provided it does not take long but is soon over, as on stage, and everyone is looking on and praising. Whereas active love is labor and perseverance.[11]

CONCLUSION

If we want to see the virtue of love, the genuine article, we must keep in mind that we will never see it all at once, in one place. We will see authentic love in the eyes of two lovers, certainly. But we will see a love with great power to touch the heart in the love of a Hospice nurse visiting the bedside of a dying person. We will see great love in the ordinary faithfulness of the parent who, day after day, week in and week out, arrives to pick up the children from school and take them home. We will see great love in the priest who is willing to spend many months in prison as a consequence for giving public witness to social injustice. We will see love in the eyes of a person who spends a lifetime in classrooms trying to instill a love for poetry, history, mathematics, music, biology, theology, or chemistry. We will see love, I tell you, in the eyes and actions of an automobile mechanic whose primary concern, year after year, is not the cars but the well-being of the people who drive them.

There is no end to what love is, and there is no end to what love means. Only remember this, that without giving and receiving love, our life is bound to be empty and without purpose. With love, no matter what else happens, life is worthwhile.

Chapter Four

ℓ

THE VIRTUE
OF PRUDENCE

The virtue of prudence is the first of the cardinal virtues. There was a time when prudence was widely admired. Indeed, parents sometimes named their daughters Prudence. Nowadays, however, prudence is a virtue frequently misunderstood. For some people the word *prudence* conjures up another word: *prude*, someone who bends over backward to be proper, modest in a puritanical way, even self-righteous, especially when it comes to anything related to sex. A "prude" is a person who would never laugh at a joke about sex.

A famous story about Winston Churchill illustrates how adept he was at deflating prudishness. England's great World War II prime minister visited America and was invited to a buffet luncheon. Cold fried chicken was served, and Churchill was fond of chicken. Returning for a second helping, he asked politely, "May I have some breast?"

"Mr. Churchill," replied the very proper hostess, "in this country we ask for white meat or dark meat." Taken aback, Churchill apologized profusely.

The next morning, however, the proper lady received

a beautiful orchid from Winston Churchill. The accompanying card read, "I would be most obliged if you would pin this on your white meat."[1]

Others understand prudence to mean being overly cautious, restrained, timid, and conservative—a person who is "buttoned down" securely and not much fun to be around. Understood this way, a prudent person is one who is so restrained that he or she would never take any chances—personal, financial, or emotional. In reality, this understanding of prudence couldn't be further from the authentic spirit of the gospel. All we need do is read a few paragraphs into the Sermon on the Mount, in the Gospel of Matthew, to recognize that the last thing a Christian virtue would do is discourage the taking of risks:

> "Blessed are the poor in spirit,
>   for theirs is the kingdom of heaven.
> "Blessed are those who mourn,
>   for they will be comforted.
> "Blessed are the meek, for they will inherit the earth.
> "Blessed are those who hunger and thirst
>   for righteousness, for they will be filled.
> "Blessed are the merciful,
>   for they will receive mercy.
> "Blessed are the pure in heart, for they will see God.
> "Blessed are the peacemakers,
>   for they will be called children of God.
> "Blessed are those who are persecuted
>   for righteousness' sake,
>   for theirs is the kingdom of heaven.
> "Blessed are you when people revile you and persecute you and utter all kinds of evil against you falsely on my account. Rejoice and be glad, for your reward is great in heaven, for in the same

way they persecuted the prophets who were before you" (5:3–12).

AUTHENTIC PRUDENCE

The virtue of authentic prudence is nothing like either of
these misunderstandings. The *Catechism of the Catholic
Church* says:

> *Prudence*...discerns our true good in every circum-
> stance and [strives] to choose the right means of
> achieving it; "the prudent man looks where he is
> going" [Proverbs 14:15].[2]

Prudence is just as likely to lead us to take a big risk
as to avoid taking one. Prudence may say, "I wouldn't do
that if I were you." But it may also say, "Go ahead and
jump; you'll never know if you don't give it a try." Prudence may advise us to climb Mount Everest, or it may
advise us to stay home. Prudence may lead us to learn to fly
an airplane, to pilot a hot-air balloon, or to put our life's
savings in a risky but potentially lucrative investment. But
prudence may also lead us to do none of these things.

In a more personal sense, when we need to use our conscience, prudence is the guide. "It is prudence," says the
Catechism, "that immediately guides the judgment of conscience."[3] The virtue of prudence gives us the ability to figure out the right thing to do in a given situation and set of
circumstances. If we are prudent, we are able to stand up
and make a decision when a decision needs to be made:

> Prudence does not answer the question: "What is
> the best way *in principle* to do the right thing?"
> Rather: "What is the best way for me, *in this situ-*

ation (i.e., in the light of these relationships and responsibilities), to do the right thing?"[4]

At such times, the words of Cardinal John Henry Newman (1801–1890), in his "Letter to the Duke of Norfolk," echo in a resounding manner throughout the Church:

> Certainly, if I am obliged to bring religion into after-dinner toasts (which indeed does not seem to be quite the thing) I shall drink—to the Pope, if you please—still to Conscience first, and to the Pope afterward.[5]

An example of prudence comes to us from the decade of the sixties, when Catholics who actively opposed the war in Vietnam had to decide what steps to take—if any— toward publicly opposing the war, steps that would clearly get them into trouble with the government of the United States. Two Catholic priests and brothers, Daniel and Philip Berrigan, and their associates, had to decide whether it was prudent to remove draft records from a Selective Service office in Catonsville, Maryland, and set them on fire outside the building as a way to protest the war. If their own safety and comfort were the primary concern, this was not a prudent choice. But if higher values were at stake, prudence would guide them to do exactly what they did, in spite of the fact that they would end up in prison for doing so. The Berrigan brothers, in their situation and circumstances, concluded that this action was a prudent choice. For a great many others it would not have been a prudent choice at all.

The virtue of prudence does not mean being impulsive. Prudent people try to "get all of their ducks in a row" before making a decision. To act in a prudent manner means investigating the issue at hand and consulting others before choosing what to do. The Berrigans did not decide on the spur of the moment to remove draft records from a government office and burn them. Their decision took months of thought, prayer, and discussion.

Prudence comes into play in many situations, from the most ordinary to the most profound. Suppose, for example, that you need a car, so you need to decide which car to buy. If you were not a prudent person, you would simply wander into the first auto dealership you happen to see and buy the first car in sight. You are not likely to go about buying a car in this manner, however, because you're probably like most people; you're far more prudent than that. Instead, you do your homework.

The virtue of prudence leads you to take certain steps before you buy. You check your bank account and review your budget to see how much you can afford to spend on a car. You do some research about makes and models of cars that are reliable and have good maintenance and safety records. You care about the impact of your driving habits on the environment, so you try to find out which cars meet or exceed established emissions standards and which ones burn fuel efficiently. You read consumer magazines to find out about the best cars to buy. You investigate the insurance rates on various models to find out how insurance expenses will add to the cost of owning a particular car. You might even consult with a mechanic you trust to see what it costs to maintain various automobiles, and to get input on the various makes and models you're considering. If you choose to buy a used car, you'll ask the mechanic to give the vehicle a bumper-to-bumper inspection to see what maintenance it needs. This is how prudence is exercised in the process of choosing what car to buy.

Prudence means using the old noodle, looking both ways before we cross the street. Prudence includes a heavy dose of good old common sense. But prudence is still more than that. Prudence has a major role to play when it comes to important moral and ethical issues. Buying a car certainly has its ethical dimensions, of course; we don't want to spend more than we can afford on a car, because that could mean that money for our basic necessities—like food, clothing, and shelter—might be scarce. Also, from an ethical vantage point, we want to choose a car that is easy on the environment. But there are moral issues of a more personal nature where prudence is essential to responsible behavior.

When it comes to moral decision making, there is a close relationship between prudence and conscience. In order to have a conscience that is alive and kicking, the virtue of prudence needs to be strong and active. One of the documents issued by the Second Vatican Council, in the mid 1960s, was the *Declaration on Religious Liberty*. This document reminds us, as did Cardinal Newman nearly a hundred years earlier, that we must follow our conscience in all that we do. It says that no one is:

> ...to be forced to act in a manner contrary to one's conscience. Nor, on the other hand, is one to be restrained from acting in accordance with one's conscience, especially in matters religious (n. 3).[6]

In his international bestseller, *Crossing the Threshold of Hope*, Pope John Paul II—not one of the most acknowledged liberals of all time—wrote:

> If a man [*sic*] is admonished by his conscience—
> even if an erroneous conscience, but one whose

voice appears to him as unquestionably true—he must always listen to it. What is not permissible is that he culpably indulge in error without trying to reach the truth.[7]

This may come as a surprise, but according to official Catholic teachings, even when one's conscience is mistaken or erroneous, no one may force a person to act contrary to conscience unless there is the potential that he or she will do serious harm to self, others, or the wider society. So, for example, we would try to stop someone from committing suicide, no matter how convinced that person might be that ending his or her own life is the "right thing to do." We would attempt to influence an employer to treat workers justly no matter how much the employer's conscience remains undisturbed with his or her current practices.

Conscience, in the normal course of affairs, may not be violated by anyone, and we are bound to follow our conscience even when it is mistaken. Since this is the way things are, what are we to do when we encounter official Church teachings or legal dictates that our conscience will not allow us to follow? For example, are we required to obey all official moral teachings of the Church and simply assume that our conscience is wrong if we disagree with the particular teaching? As we saw above, the issue of birth control is one of the most common examples of such a situation. Divorce and remarriage are other examples.

Here is where the virtue of prudence becomes a workhorse. In his monumental reference work, *Catholicism*, Father Richard McBrien outlines five principles that prudence takes into account in situations where our conscience disagrees with an official moral teaching of the Church.[8] Here is a paraphrased summary:

1. We may take it for granted that the moral teachings of the Church are normally a trustworthy
   source of wisdom and light in forming our conscience. It is important to prayerfully study and
   reflect on Church teachings. It is possible, however, that we may remain convinced that our
   conscience is correct, even though it is in conflict with an official Church teaching. In such a
   case, we not only may but *must* follow the guidance of our conscience rather than the official
   teaching of the Church.
2. None of the Church's moral teachings have ever
   been set forth as infallible. Therefore, there does
   not seem to be any instance of a conflict between a person's conscience and an infallible
   teaching of the Church.
3. No official Church teaching can ever take into
   account all possible moral situations and circumstances. Official Church teachings must be
   applied to particular unique cases. We do not
   necessarily reject the values embodied in an official Church teaching if we decide that the
   teaching is not binding on us in a particular
   unique situation.
4. Keep in mind that the Church's official teachings
   are historically conditioned. This means that what
   may have been thought to be morally wrong in
   a particular historical set of circumstances
   would be regarded as morally acceptable in
   another historical set of circumstances. One
   example of this comes to us from the Middle
   Ages when it was thought morally wrong to
   charge interest on a loan. Today, of course, it is
   not considered wrong at all.[9]

5. At the same time, no person or group can ever hope to have a complete grasp of moral truth by depending only on their own resources. We all have our limitations, and we all have our moral blind spots. We all need to be corrected from time to time. We need to rely on the moral perspectives of others, as well as our own perspectives. The Church, in which the Holy Spirit dwells, is a universal community and a major source of moral direction and leadership. The Church carries many centuries of human experience that overlaps cultural, national, and geographical boundaries. Therefore, we need to rely heavily on the moral direction offered by the Church's official teachings. In those relatively rare instances where it becomes clear that we must dissent from an official teaching, we do so with humility and regret.

It is also true, Father McBrien points out, that the virtue of prudence prompts us to listen to authorities other than the Church. We need to listen to our fellow believers in the faith community. We need to pay attention to Scripture, the findings of science, and the reflections of theologians and spiritual writers. Pope John Paul II tells us:

One is not a faithful Catholic who deliberately and systematically excludes all references to official Church teachings in making moral decisions. At the same time, "the authority of the Church, when she pronounces on moral questions, in no way undermines the freedom of conscience of Christians."[10]

PRUDENCE—LIVED AND REAL

The process of trying to figure out what to do in a particular situation and set of circumstances is traditionally called "discernment." The virtue of prudence is like a light that guides us through this process of discernment. In a very real sense, prudence is the capacity for discernment, the ability to determine what we should do. As prudent persons, we are able to discern what to do—and then do it. We gather all the information we can in order to make an informed decision or choice. We are creative and use our imagination as we consider all possible obstacles and think of ways to overcome them. We take all the information gathered and make a decision in the light of all that we have learned.

The virtue of prudence is also an important part of the traditional process of "the discernment of spirits." Although this may sound rather esoteric or spiritually sophisticated, something for those who join religious orders or become priests, such is not the case. There is nothing extraordinary about the discernment of spirits. Being a Christian means living in communion with the Spirit of God, which means being open to the Spirit and being receptive to the Spirit's influence and guidance.

It is never easy to know for sure what the Spirit wants us to do, of course; this is where the discernment of spirits comes into play. All we can do is draw conclusions from what seem to be the movements of the Spirit in our life. "One *infers* the Spirit's presence from what we...see, experience, and feel."[11] The discernment of spirits, guided by the virtue of prudence, examines all the information at our disposal and tries to see what step is the best to take, but the "information" is not limited to empirically verifiable data. In the words of Blaise Pascal, the great seventeenth-century French Catholic philosopher and mathematician, "The heart has its reasons which reason does not understand."[12]

The virtue of prudence enables us to listen to input from other people, from various authorities, and from our own life experience. Then it helps us to weigh our options before making a choice. Of course, discernment is never easy, because it is a matter of finite beings—us—relating to an infinite God. Also, we have a tendency to rationalize things in our own favor. We pay more attention, for example, to whatever supports our own self-interest, while downplaying whatever is contrary to our own self-interest. At the same time, many issues are very complicated and do not lend themselves to simple solutions.

Father McBrien explains that we can never be certain we are following the lead of the Holy Spirit, but that there are some ways we can recognize inappropriate responses. The virtue of prudence will be sensitive to these. Once again, a paraphrased summary:

1. If the discernment process does not result in the classic "fruits" of the Holy Spirit, such as love, joy, peace, patient endurance, kindness, generosity, faith, mildness, and chastity (see Galatians 5:22–23), then we are probably not truly following the inspiration of the Holy Spirit.

2. If our attempt to figure out what God wants us to do leads to doctrinal or moral positions that are obviously out of line with the doctrinal tradition of the Church and/or with widely acknowledged norms of scriptural and theological scholarship, we are probably not in line with God's will for us. Merely following our incli-

nation to "do the conservative thing" or to "do the liberal thing" can be the easy way out.

3. If a choice contributes to isolation from the faith community or encourages spiritual eccentricities, rather than nourishing the wider faith community, it is probably not consistent with being led by the Holy Spirit.

4. If we ignore important information, if we reject the advice of others who are knowledgeable and experienced in what we are trying to decide, or if our decision seems to be imposed on us rather than coming from reflection on the issue in the context of the wider faith community, then our choice is probably not "from the Holy Spirit."[13]

In all of these cases, prudence leads us to think clearly and stay prayerfully in touch with the Spirit of God leading us in the truth. The *Catechism of the Catholic Church* says:

> With the help of this virtue we apply moral principles to particular cases without error and overcome doubts about the good to achieve and the evil to avoid.[14]

Sometimes, with a kind of naive good will, people use faith as an excuse to act without prudence. One example of this is the widespread popularity of religious fundamentalism among many denominations—including Catholics. Prudence leads us to think things through, be guided by conscience, and make choices based on all the information we have been able to gather. Religious fundamentalism, on the other hand, reduces the virtue of prudence to acting with caution, a "virtue" that would never take any chances or stick its neck out regardless of the issue at hand.

Protestant fundamentalism's infallible guide is a literal or face-value reading of the Bible. Catholic fundamentalism's inerring guide is the pope, even when he is not teaching infallibly. In both Protestant and Catholic cases, fundamentalists declare that authentic faith requires them to obey blindly, without question, either a literal reading of the Bible (Protestants) or the pope's pronouncements on whatever subject (Catholics).

Thus, the virtue of prudence has no role to play unless it is interpreted as a form of cautious conservatism that will never admit the possibility that conscience may lead one to act contrary to either a fundamentalist reading of the Bible or a fundamentalist interpretation of papal teachings. (It is perfectly possible, of course, that one may end up obeying papal teachings following an intelligent, open-minded consideration of all the information.) One may suggest that for fundamentalists, faith is not an adventure and a pilgrimage but a spiritual insurance policy and a security blanket. Therefore, the virtue of prudence loses its true character as a guide that works hand-in-hand with freedom of conscience, leading us in truth.

Prudence Bears the Burden of Freedom

Prudence is the virtue that pulls the rug out from under those who long to keep their feet firmly planted on the ground. Prudence is the virtue that the Grand Inquisitor despises. In this famous story, found in Dostoevsky's classic novel, *The Brothers Karamazov*, Jesus returns to find his people dominated by a grim, gray, gaunt Grand Inquisitor, almost ninety years old, who believes with every fiber of his being that people cannot be trusted to exercise their freedom—indeed, they do not want freedom for it is more than they can bear.

In the story, Jesus returns and multitudes of people recognize him. He heals a blind man and, when he sees a little girl who has died, he brings her back to life. The Grand Inquisitor, however, is not pleased. "He scowls with his thick, gray eyebrows, and his eyes and his face darken. He stretches forth his finger and orders the guard to take him."[15]

The Inquisitor visits Jesus in prison to explain that the freedom Jesus brought the first time he came to the earth was not a freedom people could live with, so they have given up their freedom. The Inquisitor asks:

> Was it not you who so often said to them: "I want to make you free"?...For fifteen hundred years we have been at pains over this freedom, but now it is finished, and well finished...[for now] these people are more certain than ever before that they are completely free, and at the same time they themselves have brought their freedom and obediently laid it at our feet.[16]

The Church's authorities have overcome freedom, the Inquisitor says, and they have done it to "make people happy."[17] Happiness is what people want, the Inquisitor says, not freedom. The virtue of prudence, on the contrary, leads us to accept the burden of freedom and exercise that freedom by making responsible choices, the best choices possible in real situations and real circumstances. Prudence will not allow us to give up our freedom, even for the sake of certainty and in the name of faith.

Conclusion

The virtue of prudence insists that "blind obedience" is incompatible with authentic faith. When we refuse to use our own intellect and critical faculties when making moral decisions and/or when attempting to discern the will of God, we give up the freedom of Christ in return for the false security of absolute certainty and a doubt-free existence. Relative to official Church teachings on an issue such as birth control, for example, prudence may lead to obedience, or it may lead to dissent. But whether toward obedience or dissent, prudence never leads to a mindless, "knee-jerk" reaction. And always, always, prudence stands at the doors of conscience, guarding its freedom. Always.

Chapter Five

ૐ

THE VIRTUE
OF JUSTICE

T he virtue of justice gives to others what they are due or what they have a right to. Nothing could be simpler to understand than that. Of course, nothing is as simple as that, either. The question immediately pops up: what are others due or what have they a right to? This is the question upon which lawyers build their careers. This is the question that starts litigations and wars and keeps them going. People go to prison and people die every day, because of conflicts over what people are due or what they have a right to.

AUTHENTIC JUSTICE

Christianity owes a tremendous debt to Judaism for its sensitivity to justice, clearly evident in the Hebrew Scriptures, or Old Testament:

> It is to a remarkable group of men whom we call the prophets more than to any others that Western civilization owes its convictions (1) that the

future of any people depends in large part on the justice of its social order, and (2) that individuals are responsible for the social structures of their society as well as for their direct personal dealings.[1]

In the Old Testament, a "prophet" is *not* one who foretells the future. That is a modern, supermarket tabloid twist to the word, about which the Scriptures know nothing. Rather, a prophet is one who speaks for God, one who stands up and expresses God's point of view in a particular situation and set of circumstances. For the ancient Israelites, when a prophet spoke, God spoke.

Perhaps the most important event in human history, when it comes to the virtue of justice, is found in the story of Naboth (1 Kings 21:1–29) who refused to sell or trade his family's vineyard to King Ahab. In response, with the advice and help of his wife, Jezebel, King Ahab sent two "scoundrels" to falsely say that Naboth had "cursed God and the king." This amounted to charging Naboth with blasphemy and subversion, and since blasphemy was a capital crime, Naboth was stoned to death and his property became the property of the king. The consequences for Naboth were severe, but the lesson with regard to justice is clear:

> Then the word of the LORD came to Elijah the Tishbite, saying: Go down to meet King Ahab of Israel, who rules in Samaria; he is now in the vineyard of Naboth, where he has gone to take possession. You shall say to him, "Thus says the LORD: Have you killed, and also taken possession?" You shall say to him, "Thus says the LORD: In the place where dogs licked up the blood of Naboth, dogs will also lick up your blood."

Ahab said to Elijah, "Have you found me, O my enemy?" He answered, "I have found you. Because you have sold yourself to do what is evil in the sight of the LORD, I will bring disaster on you...."

When Ahab heard those words, he tore his clothes and put sackcloth over his bare flesh; he fasted, lay in the sackcloth, and went about dejectedly (21:17–21, 27).

This story is so significant for human history because it shows how someone with no worldly power—Elijah was not a priest, he had no earthly authority for what he did—stood up for a victim of injustice and accused a king, to his face, of being responsible for that injustice.

Essentially the same thing happens in the story of David and Bathsheba (2 Samuel 11:1–23; 12:1–15). "It happened, late one afternoon, when David rose from his couch and was walking about on the roof of the king's house, that he saw from the roof a woman bathing; the woman was very beautiful" (11:2). David then sent "someone" to learn the woman's identity, and word came back that she was Bathsheba, the wife of Uriah the Hittite. Later we learn that Uriah is a soldier in the army of Israel. David sent for Bathsheba, she arrived as ordered, and David "lay with her" (11:4). Later, Bathsheba realized that she had become pregnant by David, and she sent word telling him the news.

David sent for Uriah the Hittite, and when he arrived he asked him how the war was going. Then David told Uriah to return to his house and "wash your feet" (11:8). After Uriah left, David sent a gift for Uriah, but we are not told what the gift was. Uriah did not go to his house, however. Instead, he slept "at the entrance of the king's house with all the servants of his lord" (11:9). Later David received word that Uriah did not go home, so he asked Uriah why he did not do as he had been ordered. Uriah replied that with the army camped in the open field, what right did he have to go home "to eat and to drink, and to lie with my wife? As you live, and as your soul lives, I will not do such a thing" (11:11).

David decided to try again. The next day he invited Uriah back, and he gave Uriah much food and drink so that Uriah got more than a little tipsy. That night, all the same, Uriah did not return home. So the next day, in frustration, David gave Uriah a letter to take to Joab, the leader of the army. In the letter David told Joab: "Set Uriah in the forefront of the hardest fighting, and then draw back from him, so that he may be struck down and die" (11:15).

Uriah was killed in the battle, and after Bathsheba mourned for her husband, David sent for her, married her, and she gave birth to a son. "But the thing that David had done displeased the LORD" (11:27), so he sent Nathan the prophet to David, and Nathan told David a story that was an allegory for what David had done. When David heard the story, in effect he condemned himself for his actions against Uriah. Nathan said, "Why have you despised the word of the LORD, to do what is evil in his sight? You have struck down Uriah the Hittite with the sword, and have taken his wife to be your wife, and have killed him" (12:9). Fortunately, in the long run, David acknowledged his sinful injustice and repented.

In everyday life, of course, justice issues are rarely this dramatic. The need to treat people with justice boils down to the need to not steal, on the one hand, and to share with others, on the other hand.

As far as official Catholic teachings are concerned,

justice is largely an economic issue—an international economic issue. The *Catechism of the Catholic Church* says:

> *Rich nations* have a grave moral responsibility toward those which are unable to ensure the means of their development by themselves or have been prevented from doing so by tragic historical events. It is a duty in solidarity and charity; it is also an obligation in justice if the prosperity of the rich nations has come from resources that have not been paid for fairly.[2]

JUSTICE—LIVED AND REAL

The virtue of justice is both a personal and social virtue. Justice leads us to respect the rights of others and to deal with them fairly in everyday life and in the world of work. But it also leads us to be concerned about issues from capital punishment to the wages paid by companies that hire workers in other countries to manufacture products for sale both at home and abroad.

Capital punishment is a particularly thorny issue, because it seems, on the face of it, to be fair: to kill another person is to forfeit one's own right to live. As long as the standard is "an eye for an eye and a tooth for a tooth," this makes sense. But the second we shift the focus from one of "getting even" to one of Christian forgiveness, nonretaliation, reconciliation, and healing, the issue becomes not so simple. Suddenly the primary question becomes, "What would Jesus do?"

As far as official Catholic teaching is concerned, the *Catechism of the Catholic Church* allows only the tiniest possibility that capital punishment might be acceptable in a given case. It states that "the traditional teaching of the Church has acknowledged as well-founded the right and duty of legitimate public authority to punish malefactors by means of penalties commensurate with the gravity of the crime, not excluding, in cases of extreme gravity, the death penalty."[3]

To read words such as these can be unsatisfying, however. What we need is a story that can inspire us to follow an authentically Christian spirit. Such a story, and a true one, comes to us from the not so distant past, from among the Old Order Amish of Ohio.[4]

On a summer evening in 1957, two non-Amish men, Cleo Eugene Peters, age nineteen, and Michael G. Dumoulin, age twenty, got together in Holmes County, Ohio. The two young men knew each other from prison, and had agreed to meet after their release to celebrate their newfound freedom. Their idea of "celebrating" was to pick, at random, the home of Old Order Amish Paul M. and Dora J. Yoder Coblentz, in Mount Hope, Ohio. Peters and Dumoulin robbed nine dollars from the couple, molested Dora, and shot and killed Paul. Paul and Dora, true to their Amish religion, offered no resistence. Their daughter, nineteen months old, was left unharmed.

Peters and Dumoulin stole a car and fled to Illinois. There they shot a sheriff's deputy before finally being arrested. The two were returned to Ohio, where they were tried for the murder of Paul Yoder Coblentz. Peters was convicted and sentenced to death by electrocution.

Still in anguish over the murder of one of their members, the Amish community had to decide how to respond to the death sentence given Cleo Peters. Since its beginnings in the late seventeenth century, Amish doctrine had opposed capital punishment. Human life was too sacred and the possibility of repentance and reform too great for the Amish—indeed, they believe, for any Christian—

to approve of execution no matter how horrible the crime committed. But rarely had the issue of capital punishment come so close to home for the Amish. Still, God's forgiveness could not be withheld from anyone.

Amish communities as far off as Iowa wrote to Cleo Peters in prison, assuring him of their forgiveness and their prayers. Amish families invited the condemned man's parents to their homes for meals, and Amish church leaders visited him in the Lancaster County prison. At the same time, the Amish community was determined to call for a stay of execution. "Will we as Amish be blameless in the matter," one Amish man wrote, "if we do not present a written request to the authorities, asking that his [Peters'] life be spared?"[5]

The office of Governor C. William O'Neill received letters and petitions from the Amish right up until the date set for execution: November 7, 1958. Finally, just seven hours before he was scheduled to be electrocuted, Governor O'Neill commuted the sentence of Cleo Peters. Later, Amish leaders said that this experience had a profound impact on the entire Holmes County Amish community. "God has been speaking to many of us Amish people through this act," Old Order Amish leaders wrote to Peters. "We believe that God allowed this, especially to call us back to Him in the work of winning souls to His kingdom."[6]

The Amish of Holmes County, Ohio, believed that they were called to demonstrate forgiveness and peace in the real world, not merely in a world of pious theories. By acting as they did following the murder of one of their members, they showed the true meaning of justice in a world inclined to define justice as revenge.

The foundation of the virtue of authentic justice is not a concern for a superficial kind of "fair play." The best meta-

phor for justice is not a pie cut into equal parts so everyone
gets an equal piece. Rather, the foundation of the virtue of
justice is the conviction that human life is sacred. This
leaves us with a major problem in our time, however:

> As long as one is immersed in the sensory over-
> load of TV and movies that present endlessly un-
> relieved violence and killing as the unquestioned
> norm, human life is likely to be seen not only as
> cheap but worthless.[7]

The virtue of justice respects the rights of every person, not merely because it is unfair to do otherwise.
Rather, justice respects personal rights because it respects
the person, his or her sacredness as a child of God, created by God, with a right to live as fully human a life as
possible. Once we admit the sacredness of human life as
an end in itself, justice issues become self-evident. Once
we acknowledge that each and every human being, regardless of age, intelligence, or race, has a God-given value
that no one has the right to violate, then justice questions
present their own answers.

For contemporary Catholicism, the virtue of justice
has become inseparable from the qualifier, "social." For
the virtue of justice is of its very nature a social virtue.
Thus everyone has a right to be treated equally. Everyone
has a right to the same freedoms and responsibilities. In
situations where there is a history of some people being
treated unequally, however, they have a right to special
treatment until equality is established. In their 1978 document *To Do Justice*, the bishops of the United States wrote:

> In Catholic thought, social justice is not merely a
> secular or humanitarian matter. Social justice is a

reflection of God's essential respect and concern for each person to achieve his or her destiny as a child of God (no. 8).

The virtue of authentic justice cultivates respect for the dignity of all persons, for the right of all to the resources they need, and for the privilege of all to be involved in decisions that shape their lives. Once again, the Hebrew Scriptures provide considerable wisdom, as justice is identified with God's very nature: "For the LORD is a God of justice" (Isaiah 30:18b). The Old Testament also identifies justice with God's activity: "Shall not the Judge of all the earth do what is just?" (Genesis 18:25). "For you have maintained my just cause" (Psalm 9:4). Indeed, God's revelation—particularly in creation itself, in the covenant, and in the commandments—includes the establishment of justice in human lives: "The days are surely coming, says the LORD, when I will raise up for David a righteous Branch, and he shall reign as king and deal wisely, and shall execute justice and righteousness in the land" (Jeremiah 23:5).

The point of this strand of tradition in the Hebrew Scriptures is to remind us that justice is not an abstraction. Rather, through our union with God we are called to bring the spirit of justice into our lives and into our world in tangible ways. This is true not only in our personal lives, but in the knockabout world of work and careers as well. A Catholic group called Business Executives for Economic Justice authored a position paper that articulates some of the practical implications of the virtue of justice. The document is entitled, *The Buck Stops Here: Perspectives on Stewardship From Business and Professional Managers.*[8] The group wrote:

We feel that, as businesspeople, we both share the
responsibility of all Christians to be good stew-
ards and have specific responsibilities because of
our professions.

This position paper defines "stewardship" as "people
extending themselves, helping make possible opportunities for others, enriching their lives and sensitivities by
exercising their talents, resources, and energies."[9] In other
words, stewardship is a way of living the virtue of justice
in the world of business.

The Buck Stops Here addresses five areas of responsibility for business and professional managers: the stewardship of people, products and services, community, the
environment, and the social fabric.

Stewardship of people: For business and professional
managers, stewardship of people "includes—not always
in this order—the care and development of investors/
owners, employees, clients/customers, suppliers, and even,
at times….competitors."[10]

A savings and loan company gives us a good example
of stewardship of people when it "experienced a prolonged
downsizing," and the possibility of government takeover
became very real. The senior vice president for human
resources lived the virtue of justice in his work by making sure that "investor value was restored, customers
continued to be well served," and most affected employees were either retrained for new jobs with the savings
and loan or helped to find work with other companies.[11]
Later, this savings and loan was purchased at a price that
gave shareholders a profit yet left the company intact as
a local lender and major employer.

Stewardship of products and services: Living the virtue of justice through stewardship of products and services means maintaining a concern for how products and services are produced, marketed, and distributed. For example, a publishing company sold a self-help book for twenty-five years, and it was still selling very well. The publisher realized, however, that much of the material in the book was out of date, so a mere revision of the book was out of the question. Instead, the publisher commissioned an entirely new book, at the risk of losing the marketing success of the original book. The publisher spent money to fix something that, in terms of its marketability, wasn't broken. Yet concern for justice and for providing accurate, up-to-date information to the readership prompted the publisher to take the risk.

Stewardship of the community: Living the virtue of justice through stewardship of the community includes local, national, and international communities. It means maintaining a lively concern about finding solutions for social problems, and it means using business skills not only for our own business enterprises, but for other institutions in communities as well. This includes paying a fair share of community expenses, including taxes.

It is not uncommon for companies to negotiate large tax decreases in return for locating their business in particular cities or neighborhoods. One company bought a bankrupt manufacturing business, then voluntarily negotiated a large *increase* in its tax assessment. This company could have kept its taxes about the same for a long time by playing various legal games. But the company was located in a small town where the school district was finding it increasingly difficult to stay operating. Instead of being guided by self-interest for the short run, this company's new owners met with community leaders to help provide the money needed for education. "We believe that this was an investment in the community and will have long-term benefits for our company," said the CEO of the company.[12]

Stewardship of the environment: The virtue of justice also has an environmental dimension. A business that lives the virtue of justice is willing to pay the costs of protecting the environment as a legitimate part of doing business. This business will go beyond the minimum requirements of the law in order to do what's best for the environment for decades to come. For example, instead of being careful about launching a new product line while continuing to sell existing products, a company that manufactures paper products decided to switch entirely to 100 percent recycled paper for all of its products. The company's managers believed that risking damage to the environment was unjust. They rejected the popular opinion that there would not be enough recycled paper available, that what there was would be of inferior quality, and that it would be more expensive than new paper. Instead, this company developed the new products and successfully marketed them.[13]

Stewardship of the social fabric: A business that lives the virtue of justice cares for the social fabric of the wider community through "philanthropy, education, human relations, civil rights, and works of mercy."[14] The virtue of justice requires both smaller and larger companies to give not only financial support to good causes, but to share business skills and organizational experience to help deal with social problems. For example, an investment management company gives 80 percent of its charitable contributions to organizations in which its employees are involved as volunteers. The company offers its donations equally to all its employees, regardless of their position in the company. "We follow our employees' good work and leadership with our cash," said an executive vice president of this company.[15]

The virtue of justice has a place not only in the world of business, of course. Justice is also needed in the institutional dealings of the Church, from parish to diocese to the national and international levels. Sometimes Church leaders find it easier to preach about justice than to live it. But the Church-as-employer has the same responsibilities to its employees that secular employers have. These responsibilities include offering medical plans, retirement plans and, of course, fair pay.

JUSTICE TEMPERS LAW WITH COMPASSION AND FORGIVENESS

Like the other virtues, justice is ultimately a matter of the heart, even though it must show itself in practical, everyday, "real-world" ways if it is to be more than a collection of fine-sounding words. Justice in the heart means being deeply convinced that other people are just as human as I am, children of God—just like me. Justice in the heart means tempering law with compassion and forgiveness.

Although we tend to think of justice first of all in relation to other people, justice is also a virtue in relation to God. According to the *Catechism of the Catholic Church*, justice is "the moral virtue that consists in the constant and firm will to give their due *to God and neighbor*" (no. 1807, emphasis added).

But what does justice with regard to God mean? What does it mean to give God his due? As the *Catechism* also explains, this refers to what is sometimes called "the virtue of religion." To call religion a "virtue" means that we practice our religion as a source of power and strength. We live the virtue of justice with regard to God by being faithful to our Catholic faith. We do this by being prayerful, faithful people in our everyday lives, in our homes and with our families; by celebrating the Eucharist on Sundays; by participating in a community of faith; by observing our Catholic traditions; and by giving witness to our faith—above all by our actions—in the wider secular communities to which we belong.

Failure to live the virtue of justice with regard to God are not as uncommon as we might think. The *Catechism of the Catholic Church* discusses three possibilities (nos. 2119–2121). Among such are "tempting God," which is evident among sectarian Christians who take the words of Scripture literally, sell all their possessions, then wait for God to take care of them.

Another example of "tempting God" is found in those Christian sects that take literally the words of Jesus in the Gospel of Mark: "And these signs will accompany those who believe....they will pick up snakes in their hands, and if they drink any deadly thing, it will not hurt them" (16:17–18). Such sects often include the handling of poisonous snakes and the drinking of poison in their worship gatherings, all this to prove that their faith is genuine. From the Catholic perspective, such actions violate the virtue of justice by "tempting God," by putting his goodness and power to the test, by trying to force him to cause miracles to happen.

Another failure to live the virtue of justice with regard to God is called "sacrilege." This means insulting or being disrespectful toward the sacraments and other liturgical actions, as well as persons, places, or things consecrated to God. Catholicism views sacrilege as a grave sin, particularly when committed against the Eucharist, because in this sacrament the whole person of the risen Christ is "substantially present for us."[16] To use the traditional phrase, in the Eucharist the risen Christ is present "body and blood, soul and divinity." Therefore, to insult or be disrespectful toward the Eucharist is sacrilegious and a violation of the virtue of justice with regard to God.

"Simony" is another example of failure to live the virtue of justice with regard to God. This refers to the buying or selling of spiritual things. The term comes from the name of the magician in the Acts of the Apostles— Simon—who wanted to buy the spiritual power he witnessed in the apostles. "Give me also this power so that anyone on whom I lay my hands may receive the Holy Spirit," Simon says. "But Peter said to him, 'May your silver perish with you, because you thought you could obtain God's gift with money!'" (8:19–20).

Does this mean that no one should give a stipend to a priest or deacon who, for example, presides at a wedding or funeral, or that no one should give an offering when asking that a Mass be said for a particular intention? No. The point is, it is not possible to possess and use spiritual goods as if they could be owned. The material support of the clergy is another matter. Quoting the Church's Code of Canon Law, the *Catechism of the Catholic Church* declares:

> "The minister should ask nothing for the administration of the sacraments beyond the offerings defined by the competent authority, always being careful that the needy are not deprived of the help

of the sacraments because of their poverty"
(Canon 848). The competent authority determines
these "offerings" in accordance with the principle
that the Christian people ought to contribute to
the support of the Church's ministers. "The la-
borer deserves his food" (Matthew 10:10).[17]

CONCLUSION

The virtue of justice is a spiritual and personal virtue,
one that enables us to seek the good of others even at our
own sacrifice, knowing that the good of others is, in reality, our own good as well. It is also a virtue that empowers us to practice our religion, not as a sideline or spiritual hobby but as a way of life, giving our Creator the
worship due him, which is, again, for our own good.

How important is the virtue of justice? Saint Augustine of Hippo, some fifteen hundred years ago, said it as
plainly as anyone ever could: "Let justice be done though
the world perish."

Chapter Six

?

THE VIRTUE
OF FORTITUDE

Row upon row of emaciated prisoners, dressed in drab, black-and-white striped prison uniforms, stood in ragged ranks. It was July 30, 1941, and the place was Auschwitz, the Nazi death camp in Poland. The camp commander, Herr Kommandant Fritsch, had announced earlier that someone had escaped from the camp. After three hours of standing, Kommandant Fritsch told the prisoners to return to their miserable quarters in Block 14.

Steaming hot soup was brought to the men, but they were not allowed to eat. Rather, the soup kettle was placed in the cell block, its aroma driving the starved prisoners frantic. Once the prisoners were crazed with their need for food, the Nazi guards poured the soup down a drain.

At six o'clock the next morning, all the prisoners in the camp were once again lined up. Kommandant Fritsch announced in a loud voice that because the man who escaped had not been found, ten prisoners would be chosen to die in the starvation bunker. He explained further that the next time someone escaped, twenty would die in the same manner. Fritsch then dismissed all the prisoners except those from Block 14, the block from which the prisoner had escaped. The men were ordered to stand at attention in the hot prison yard for several hours—without food or water. Soon the men began to faint, one by one. At about 3:30 in the afternoon the guards gave the prisoners from Block 14 some rest and brought them some tasteless soup and water.

As the sun began to go down, the Nazi commander began to choose the ten that would die by starvation. Slowly, Kommandant Fritsch walked back and forth among the ranks of prisoners. With no reason for his choices, he selected the men and ordered them to step forward and march to the starvation bunker. One of Fritsch's choices was a man named Francis Gajowniczek, who began crying. "How I pity my wife and children whom I'm leaving as orphans," he said.

Suddenly one man left his place in line, moved toward Kommandant Fritsch, and somehow was able to kiss the Kommandant's hand. Repelled, Fritsch asked his translator, "What does this Polish swine want?"

"I want to die in place of one of the condemned," said Maximilian Kolbe, prisoner 16670.

"Why?" Fritsch asked.

Kolbe replied, "I am an old man, Sir, and good for nothing. My life is no longer of use to anyone."

"In whose place do you wish to die?" the Kommandant asked.

"For the one with the wife and children," Kolbe said, indicating Francis Gajowniczek.

No one had ever stepped out of line in such a situation, for it would have meant certain death; the guards would have shot immediately. Not this time, however. For some reason, the exchange between Maximilian Kolbe and Kommandant Fritsch took place with no interruption.

Fritsch saw before him a starving man in his forties who looked much older due to his time in the camp. Never before in this camp of death and suffering had anyone volunteered to give his life for another

"Who are you?" Fritsch asked.

"I am a Catholic priest," Father Kolbe said quietly.

In the opinion of the Nazis, only Jews were lower than Catholic priests. So when Fritsch heard the word "priest," he immediately agreed to Father Kolbe's proposal. The Nazi guards herded the condemned prisoners into their death cell, Bunker 11. Naturally the prisoners were ready to despair. Gradually, however, Maximilian Kolbe helped them keep up their faith in God. Father Kolbe urged them to turn to the Blessed Mother, Mary, to keep from becoming the despairing, anguished creatures the Nazis wanted them to become.

As the hours passed, Father Kolbe prayed aloud so the other prisoners could hear his voice and join in. When the other prisoners cried out in their suffering, he inspired them to calm down. Each day, when the guards came to do their inspection, they found Father Kolbe leading the prisoners in prayer, and only the shouts of the guards would make them stop. Father Kolbe was the only prisoner who asked for nothing and did not complain.

After one week, the prisoners were so weakened they could only say their prayers in a whisper. While the others lay on the floor, helpless, Father Kolbe greeted the guards each day standing or kneeling, his face still serene. One of the guards said, "This priest is a real man. I never saw one like him here before."

Finally only four prisoners remained alive. Because the Nazis wanted the bunker for other prisoners, Fritsch ordered the prison physician, Dr. Bock, to inject the remaining prisoners with carbolic acid. The date was August 14, 1941.

Later, when the prisoner assigned to remove the bodies entered Father Kolbe's cell, he found the priest sitting on the floor, leaning against the wall, his eyes still open. His body was still clean and even seemed to have a subtle glow about it, while the other prisoners lay on the floor dirty, their faces showing signs of despair.

On August 15, 1941, Father Maximilian Kolbe's body was cremated in the horrible ovens of Auschwitz. On October 10, 1982, Pope John Paul II canonized Saint Maximilian Kolbe in a centuries'-old ritual in St. Peter's Basilica in Rome. Without question, Maximilian Kolbe lived the virtue of authentic fortitude to a heroic degree.[1]

AUTHENTIC FORTITUDE

The virtue of fortitude certainly includes courage, but it is broader than that. "Fortitude may be defined as that quality of character through which its possessor is enabled to endure hardships and to overcome fears that would tend to deflect an individual from the pursuit of the aims of a humanly and Christian good life."[2] Fortitude means standing firm in hope against all pressures to despair, even in the face of death itself. In times of suffering, emptiness, and uncertainty, fortitude offers strength against fear. In the gospels, Jesus frequently urges his followers to be courageous and not be afraid:

> "Do not fear those who kill the body but cannot kill the soul; rather fear him who can destroy both soul and body in hell. Are not two sparrows sold

for a penny? Yet not one of them will fall to the ground apart from your Father. And even the hairs of your head are all counted. So do not be afraid; you are of more value than many sparrows" (Matthew 10:28–31).

Fortitude is not just the physical courage shown, for example, by soldiers or sailors in battle. It includes the spiritual and moral courage that makes it possible for us to put up with the disapproval of others in response to our efforts on behalf of social justice. Fortitude also includes the patience and perseverance needed to be faithful to our vocation as an artist of whatever kind. The virtue of fortitude makes it possible for us to resist an inclination to run away from danger, but it also enables us to avoid taking foolish or unnecessary risks.

In Catholic tradition, there are two main actions performed by fortitude—endurance and attack.[3] Endurance is not a passive submission to danger and suffering. Rather, it is a holding strongly to the good while, at the same time, refusing to give in to pain and/or fear. Saint Maximilian Kolbe is an exceptional example of fortitude and endurance.

Fortitude's second action is attack. Fortitude expresses itself by attacking evil and blocking its progress, if this can be done by reasonable means. "When attack stems from motives that are not selfish or wrong, it has sometimes been called 'holy anger.'"[4] Generally speaking, endurance has been more common than attack, and better understood. From the time of the early Christian martyrs, for example, endurance has demanded great bravery. Attack is a legitimate form of fortitude, of course, and it is found in the lives of those who oppose social and economic injustice and in the example of those who promote—by reasonable, nonviolent means—respect for life by opposing abortion and euthanasia.

Less spectacular examples of fortitude include a quiet dedication to love for neighbor when that love is not returned. We also see fortitude in a faithful, patient persistence in prayer when God does not seem to respond. The same may be said of those who are courageously persistent about participation in Twelve Step recovery groups. In such cases, and many more from the everyday world, the virtue of fortitude enables us, with the grace of God, to choose and act on whatever is good, to choose what gives life, even in the face of anxiety, fear, threats of harm, and even death itself.

We can nurture fortitude in ourselves by learning about what is good, by spending time with good people, and by following Jesus' instruction to love God with our whole self—which calls for daily prayer—and to love our neighbor as we love ourselves. In other words, fortitude comes, first and foremost, from rooting our heart in the gospel so that our deepest beliefs govern our choices at all times. As long as we keep the goals of the gospel uppermost in our mind and heart, we will act with fortitude when the time for fortitude comes.

In his song "Across the Milky Way," singer/songwriter John Stewart states one of the greatest mysteries of fortitude: to be courageous sometimes means we need to face directly what we are afraid of, or whatever it is that would lead us to act in a less than courageous manner. "If you are lost as in a dream / and cannot find your way, / all the reasons you are lost / will guide you on your way."[5] In other words, the virtue of fortitude may require us to look directly at whatever it is that is frightening us, and to act in a courageous manner in spite of that fear. Eleanor Roosevelt said:

You gain strength, courage and confidence by every experience in which you really stop to look fear in the face. You are able to say to yourself, "I lived through this horror. I can take the next thing that comes along." ...You must do the thing you think you cannot do.[6]

FORTITUDE—LIVED AND REAL

Oddly enough, the virtue of fortitude sometimes shows itself without us even recognizing it as such. People act with heroic fortitude almost every day, and when they receive recognition, the response is quite often, "I just did what had to be done." A famous true story of this kind involves John F. Kennedy. During World War II, JFK was an officer in the U.S. Navy and commander of a PT boat in the South Pacific. In August 1943, in Blackett Strait in the Solomon Islands, a Japanese destroyer rammed Kennedy's PT boat and sank it. Kennedy and some of his men managed to swim to a nearby island only to discover that it was inhabited by the Japanese. He and another officer swam to yet another island, where they talked some of the natives into carrying a message to other American forces, who later rescued Kennedy and his crew. Years later Kennedy's comment on his heroism was typical of many people who act with fortitude: "It was involuntary. They sank my boat."[7]

Indeed, true stories of real people in real-life situations living authentic fortitude provide us with tremendous inspiration. An anonymous French priest gives us another good example. During World War II, this priest complied with a directive from the Vichy government—the puppet government installed by the Nazis—to instruct the people of his parish about the attitude they were required to have toward the Nazis. The priest did the legal minimum in this regard and then he went on with his sermon, in which he denounced Nazi paganism, aggression, and injustice. "No true peace can live without liberty," he said, "otherwise it means only tyranny, hatred, and revolt." Having thus spoken, the priest left the pulpit, but not before saying to the congregation: "If anyone among you wishes to report me to the Germans, tell them they will find me in my presbytery."[8]

Stories such as these are plentiful, and they serve an important purpose: they inspire those of us who live ordinary lives to live the virtue of authentic fortitude in our own small ways, in our own small places. No one should think that fortitude is limited to heroes in heroic situations. One of the best known examples of someone who lived the virtue of fortitude in quiet and hidden ways is Saint Thérèse of Lisieux (1873–1897). A French Carmelite nun who grew up something of a "spoiled child" in comfortable circumstances, Thérèse Martin entered the cloistered Carmelite convent at Lisieux on April 9, 1888. She was barely fifteen years old. From that day until her death from tuberculosis nine years and five months later on September 30, 1897, Thérèse lived the regulated life of the Carmelite nuns, which began each day at 4:45 A.M. and ended at 10:30 or 11:00 P.M.

It was an ordinary life, really, even humdrum—the days filled with menial work and prayer. Yet Thérèse lived the virtue of fortitude to a heroic degree. She spoke of her struggle to be patient with other nuns who accidentally splashed soapy water on her while they did the community's laundry by hand. She wrote about trembling with impatient rage as she resisted the desire to turn around and shoot an angry glance at a nun who rattled her rosary beads during community prayer times.

In her famous autobiography, *Story of a Soul*, Thérèse wrote that she wanted to "seek out a means of going to heaven by a little way, a way that is very straight, very short, and totally new."[9] This she did primarily by living the virtue of fortitude. It took great courage and endurance to make the ordinary little things of everyday life the stuff of heroic love and union with God. It took the virtue of authentic fortitude to stick with a plan to live a heroic faith without doing anything heroic! Thérèse believed with all her heart that "this moment now, which she seems at the same time to declare is illusory, is almost infinitely worthwhile."[10]

Thérèse saw each minute as a kind of window on eternity. She realized that whatever that minute called her to do—regardless of how ordinary it might be—it offered her an opportunity to be one with God's will for her. But to follow through on this belief, to use her minutes well, she had to have the virtue of fortitude, the strength to act as if what she believed were true, not just a mind game. The depth of Thérèse's belief in this reality is evident in a canticle she wrote:

> My life is but an instant, a mere passing hour,
> My life escapes and flies away, this single day,
>   no other.
> You know, O Lord: To love you on this earth,
> I have this day, no other!...
>
> What matters, Lord, a future bleak?
> Beg you for tomorrow, I shall not, cannot!...
> But keep my heart pure, put me in your shade
> Just for this day, no other.

Soon I shall fly to sing your praise,
And leave this day, no other.
Then I shall play the angels' lyre,
And no longer say that on my soul it sets,
This day, no other.

But on my soul it shines:
Your everlasting day, all other![11]

Thérèse compared herself to a little flower, which is why those devoted to her often refer to her as "the little flower." Over the years, however, this image has taken on sentimental implications that Thérèse herself never intended. Rather, when she used the image of a little flower, she was talking about the virtue of fortitude. She had in mind something like what Saint Paul says:

For God's foolishness is wiser than human wisdom, and God's weakness is stronger than human strength. Consider your own call, brothers and sisters: not many of you were wise by human standards, not many were powerful, not many were of noble birth. But God chose what is foolish in the world to shame the wise; God chose what is weak in the world to shame the strong (1 Corinthians 1:25–27).

The image of a little flower has nothing to do with a sappy sentimental spirituality. Rather, it is an image of fortitude in weakness, the paradox at the heart of the Christian life, in fact.

Saint Thérèse of Lisieux is one of the modern era's greatest champions of the virtue of fortitude in everyday life. She saw the infinite value of each day and taught a spirituality based on the fortitude needed to act with love and faith in the utterly ordinary challenges and joys of everyday life. This is the virtue of fortitude lived in a way that everyone can understand.

Fortitude is the virtue that enables us to be faithful to our vows, promises, and commitments. Fortitude, for example, is the virtue upon which a lasting marriage is built. Fortitude is the virtue that makes it possible for parents to continue caring for and guiding their children through good times and bad. It takes fortitude for a priest to be faithful to his vocation, and it takes fortitude for a vowed religious brother or sister to persevere in fidelity to his or her religious vows in times when everything in the Church and in religious life seems so uncertain, so unpredictable. The virtue of fortitude gives each of us the inner spiritual power to remain faithful, one day at a time.

Rebbe Nachman of Breslov (1772–1810) was a great Jewish spiritual seeker and one of the most frequently quoted of the Hasidic spiritual masters. His main message revolved around the importance and value of fortitude. Never lose hope, he said over and over again. Instead, find joy and cause for happiness in everything that happens to you. Here are a few of Rebbe Nachman's aphorisms:[12]

I will ignore tomorrow and all future tomorrows— today is all there is!

Growing spiritually can be like a roller coaster ride. Take comfort in the knowledge that the way down is only preparation for the way up.
In the early stages of your spiritual journey, it may seem that Heaven is rejecting you and spurning

all your efforts. Stay on course! Don't give up. In
time, all barriers will disappear.

Be strong willed and stubborn if you want to get
closer to God. How else will you survive all the
difficulties that are sure to come your way?

Always remember: You are never given an obstacle
you cannot overcome.

All of these aphorisms from Rebbe Nachman encour-
age the virtue of fortitude. They advise the spiritual seeker
to be patient, courageous, humble, and persistent.

Rebbe Nachman encourages us to draw on fortitude
in our spiritual life. It takes fortitude, for example, to be
faithful to a daily discipline of prayer, regardless of the
kind of prayer we find most worthwhile. It's not that everyone should try to live like those who inhabit monas-
teries. Quite the contrary; we ordinary folk who thrash
about in the ordinary world live too busy an existence to
try to maintain the rhythm of prayer and work that char-
acterizes the monastic day. All the same, we can select
certain devotional prayers that, among other things, help
maintain a faith perspective and awareness in the course
of our everyday lives.[13]

Today's Catholics are leery at times about devotions,
because in "the old days," prior to the Second Vatican
Council, devotional prayers often seemed to be more important than the liturgy. Sometimes they seemed to smack
of superstition and simplistic faith. As a result, many
Catholics eschewed the whole idea of devotional prayer.
Unfortunately, the baby went out with the bath water.

But devotional prayer is important to an everyday
practice of our faith. We do well to choose devotions that

support and enrich our intimacy with God, and to stick with those devotions through thick and thin—which is where the virtue of fortitude becomes important to our prayer life.[14]

When we are new to regular prayer, it isn't difficult to remain faithful to our routine. Once the novelty wears off, however, it's another story. It takes fortitude to remain faithful to a daily prayer schedule. Whether we decide to pray the rosary or some other form of Marian devotion, pray parts of the Liturgy of the Hours, or pray a devotion to a favorite saint, fidelity to our daily discipline of prayer is the most important thing.

The word *discipline* is not too strong a word here. For the practice of daily prayer must be a discipline if it is to have a real impact on our life. This is why the virtue of fortitude is important in our prayer lives. Devotional prayer, by its very nature, has an affective quality to it. But we cannot rely on feelings to keep us going with prayer. Rather, love alone keeps us faithful to a daily prayer regimen. Here, of course, "love" is not a feeling or emotion. Rather, this is love, as Saint Thomas Aquinas described it, that is actually an act of the will that seeks openness to God's loving presence and his action in our life.

Praying leads to a desire to pray more. In other words, prayer itself nourishes the virtue of fortitude, which supports a dedication to daily prayer. Because prayer is not a magic way to make sure that all things go as we think they should, we need fortitude. Consider the following:

> Living with God demands courage. When things go well, it is easy to assume God is with us. But when things go poorly, doubts arise. God never

really abandons us, but we forget God's constant presence. And we pay the consequences of anxiety, confusion, distress—not because God wants this but because these are the natural results of turning away from God's truth, God's way, and God's life, all of which require courage.[15]

FORTITUDE BELIEVES
IN THE LIGHT

The virtue of fortitude is the virtue that leads us through the dark night, over the bumpy road, through those times when everything seems bound to turn out for the worst. The virtue of fortitude believes in the light even when the night is darkest. The virtue of fortitude gives us a swift kick when we need it most. It says, "Stand up, start moving, stop feeling sorry for yourself, stick your neck out if necessary, and take a chance. Risk everything—or what looks like everything—if it looks like that is your only option." The virtue of fortitude reminds us that even death itself is nothing but a new beginning, so there is nothing needed but trust.

Let us not take this line of reflection as obvious, however. Let us not allow ourselves to nod away, ready to give in to trite pieties. To say that it takes fortitude to remain faithful—to a daily regimen of devotional prayer or meditation, to our commitments, to our vocations—is to say something like, "It takes strength to swim the English Channel." This fortitude is so necessary because the world we inhabit does not support such a project, it's as simple as that. Just the opposite, in fact, is true: the inclination to live our daily lives as if there is no God is difficult to ignore, difficult in the extreme. Consider this:

One of the most consequential ideas embedded in modern institutions and traditions and habits of thought is theological. Stated bluntly, it is the assumption that even if God exists he is largely irrelevant to the real business of life. To put this somewhat more tactfully, contemporary society and culture so emphasize human potential and human agency and the immediate practical exigencies of the here and now, that we are for the most part tempted to go about our daily business in this world without giving God much thought. Indeed, we are tempted to live as though God did not exist, or at least as if his existence did not practically matter.[16]

Here is the situation we live in: a social and cultural environment that is taken for granted by everyone, therefore cultivated by the mass media, and even—believe it or not—in some ways taken for granted by parish communities. Therefore to dedicate ourselves to daily devotional prayer or meditation, commitments, and vocations requires the virtue of fortitude—big-time!

CONCLUSION

Fortitude has both personal and social expressions if we are to live our Catholic faith in today's world. Fortitude is needed in the rare situation where true heroism is called for, but it is needed far more frequently in the course of ordinary, everyday life. The virtue of fortitude is the virtue that makes it possible for us to live our life and our faith authentically and with some degree of steadfastness.

§

Chapter Seven

THE VIRTUE
OF TEMPERANCE

The virtue of temperance got a bad reputation during the late nineteenth and early twentieth centuries. *Temperance* became synonymous with being a teetotaler, a person who abstains completely from alcoholic beverages.

The National Woman's Christian Temperance Union was founded in Cleveland, Ohio, in 1874. Members of this group, among whom was Carrie Nation, the famous tavern-smashing temperance advocate, employed educational, social, and political means to promote legislation. During the 1880s the organization spread to other countries and, in 1883, the World's Woman's Christian Temperance Union was formed.

In fact, the virtue of temperance is not about abstaining completely from anything. Rather, the virtue of temperance helps us to respond to all our appetites with moderation. It helps us to become balanced, well integrated persons. Temperance sees our appetites and instincts not as ends in themselves but as means to a greater end. The virtue of temperance disciplines our desires, moving them toward what is good for our relationships with God and others. This includes all our inclinations whether sensual, spiritual, or intellectual.

As so often is the case, G. K. Chesterton, the great early twentieth-century convert to Catholicism, spoke words witty and wise on the subject of teetotalers and temperance:

> The teetotaler has chosen a most unfortunate phrase for the drunkard when he says that the drunkard is making a beast of himself. The man who drinks ordinarily makes nothing but an ordinary man of himself. The man who drinks excessively makes a devil of himself. But nothing connected with a human and artistic thing like wine can bring one nearer to the brute life of nature. The only man who is, in the exact and literal sense of the words, making a beast of himself is the teetotaler.[1]

One way to view temperance is to see it as the inner guide that leads us in the direction of selfless self-preservation.[2] Temperance understands and respects our sensual instincts as means to union with God and neighbor. The point is that the body is not the enemy of the soul but its ally. Body and soul are meant to be the best of friends. In fact, the greatest spiritual guides down through the centuries have always called for moderation as the best path, moderation as much in eating, for example, as in fasting.

AUTHENTIC TEMPERANCE

The virtue of temperance might well be renamed the virtue of moderation. Temperance teaches us to be moderate in all things, to refrain from going to extremes, no matter what behavior is in question. To abandon moderation, or temperance, is to give ourselves over to the forces of disintegration. To follow the lead of any of the human appetites, whenever we experience that appetite, is to act in an unbalanced and unhealthy manner. It is not good *for me*, for example, to eat every time I feel like eating—therefore it is not good *for my relationship with God*, who wants me to remain healthy for the sake of his service. Eating every time I experience a desire for food will eventually affect my relationships with my family and friends as well.

Living in a highly affluent society, we need the virtue of temperance in numerous ways. Here are but a few examples:

- Consumption with regard for our environment. We need to use the things we buy and the earth's resources responsibly. We need to take seriously the need to recycle and re-use. Temperance reminds us to care about the impact of our consumer habits on our home, the earth.
- Gambling responsibly. If we gamble at all, for recreational purposes, we need to use only money we can truly afford to lose because the odds are overwhelming that lose it is exactly what we will do. We need to withhold our heart from the gambling experience whether we are in a casino or in a convenience store to buy a lottery ticket.

- Smoking. Through youthful foolishness, a person may be so addicted to nicotine as to find it physically and psychologically impossible to quit. Still, we can at least temper our consumption of a self-destructive drug that has no redeeming qualities. Nicotine is a highly addictive drug that is guaranteed to damage our lungs, heart, and brain, lead to a slow, painful death (or at least shorten our life), and render us unpleasant for other people to be around because it makes us stinky, smelly people and fouls the air other people have to breath. (Okay, I admit that I would like to see the cigarette companies blasted off the face of the earth—a feeling I need to temper.)

- Body image. Exercise for good health is virtuous. Getting carried away with "working out" is not. Dressing comfortably and modestly is virtuous. Becoming a "fashion plate" is not. Spending inordinate amounts of money on trying to look young and fit is not virtuous. Cosmetic surgery merely to look younger than you are has questionable value, especially if you can't afford it. It's virtuous to accept your own mortality.

- Spiritual gluttony. Some people eat too much. Some people spend way too much time on explicitly religious activities. Most Catholics today could use more devotional prayer, but temperance means putting a limit on it, not spending hours a day praying or hours a day in church lighting candles. God says to those who pray too much: Get a life!

- Television watching. Hoo boy, is this a biggie. It's difficult to imagine that people are actually watching television every minute they have the set turned on. Still, surveys report that the average home has a television set on seven, count 'em, seven hours a day! Temperance means to shut the darn thing off, for heaven's sake. Again, God says: Get a life!
- Computer use. This is a relatively new phenomenon. "Surfing the net" can become addictive. Playing computer games can be habit-forming. Participation in "chat rooms" can get out of hand. E-mailing far and wide can get *way* out of hand. The virtue of temperance asks us to remember that there are only so many hours in the day and, hey, when was the last time you kissed your spouse, hugged your kids, or read a good book?
- Hobbies and recreation. It's fine to collect stamps, sea shells, old gasoline pumps, baseball cards, tea cozies, or whatever. It's fine to write triolets for a hobby. It's fine to have a cabin at the lake, it's fine to spectate at baseball, football, basketball, soccer, and/or hockey games. But put a limit on it. The virtue of temperance might lead you to buy a recreational vehicle to take vacations in, but temperance asks you if you need *two* RVs. No hobby or form of recreation should dominate a person's whole life, even if you are retired. There are less fortunate people out there who need you!
- Work, work, work. Temperance has a big job in some people's lives, getting them to rethink the wisdom of climbing the corporate ladder,

or working sixty hours a week because over-time pays so well. As the old song says, you work your fingers to the bone, and what do you get? Bony fingers! The lifestyles of the rich and famous are vastly overrated. What matters is what's going on in your heart. What matters is what's going on in your relationships.

- Stress as a way of life. The virtue of temper-ance reminds us to give our heart a break, to eliminate some of the sources of stress, not add more to the collection. If someone calls asking you to volunteer you can ask yourself one ques-tion: Will doing this increase or decrease my stress level? And the choice is yours.

The virtue of temperance applies to every dimension of life, and that includes sex. If every time I experience sexual stimulation or arousal I insist on having sex with my spouse that will have a negative impact on our mar-riage. But it will also have a negative impact on my own well-being. My life will become chaotic if I allow many of my appetites or inclinations to lead me around by the nose. A person who allows his or her appetites to call the shots is no longer free.

We said that the virtue of temperance leads in the direction of selfless self-preservation. Here is one example of what this means. It is true to say that a Christian is one who is dedicated to serving or caring for others. But the virtue of temperance moderates the number of hours per week that even the most dedicated servant of the poor, for example, puts into doing whatever he or she does to serve the poor. There comes a time when the one who cares for others must take time for self—for the sake of others!

If I am to have the energy I need to care for others I must take time for leisure myself. It will do no one any good in the long run if I work sixty or seventy hours a week "serving the poor." On the contrary, with a schedule like this, sooner or later I will collapse, probably sooner rather than later. Before long, I will become less and less effective because I will be scraping the bottom of the psychic and spiritual barrel in my attempts to help others. Temperance tells me to get some balance into my life, to limit the number of hours I work each day, to find time for leisure, for prayer, to engage in some activities I enjoy, to make a retreat, to read a book, to listen to music, see a good movie, or attend a concert or play.

Temperance also reminds you that you can't share what you do not have. You can't share a new idea if you don't take the time to read a book or attend a lecture. You can't share your love for God if you don't take time to be with God in prayer or meditation. You can't work hard for others if you don't get the rest you need so you will have the energy to work hard for others.

In this case, the virtue of temperance taps you on the shoulder and says, "Hey. Everything does not depend on you and your efforts. Give it a rest. You did all you could, now give it a rest." It's a simpleminded slogan, but it carries some truth as well: "Let go and let God."

Another way to look at the virtue of temperance is to see it as having to do with your relationship with yourself, and *balance* is the ideal to strive for. Temperance helps us deal creatively and well with the "balancing act" of life, and there is a distinctively Christian perspective on this that is unique compared to that of the ancient Greek philosophers.

Plato thought of human sensuous craving as "an ugly brute of a horse" which had to be controlled by the "chari-

oteer," that is, the human intellect.[3] The Stoic philosophers also saw the appetites as needing to be dominated
and controlled by reason. From a different perspective,
however, the early Christian theologians understood temperance as part of a "grace-full" way of life, "as a way of
participating in the death and Resurrection of Christ."[4]
They saw the human person as having to "die to self" by
not giving in to every inclination of the human appetites.
Exercising this form of control over oneself, they taught,
would lead to new life in the Spirit.

Saint Thomas Aquinas, however, taught that it is virtuous not to *repress* the desire for sensual pleasure, but
to *temper* it for the sake of a deeper humanity. Temperance is positive, he said, not negative. Temperance humanizes the pleasures of eating, drinking, and sex. Lover
of intellectual analysis that he was, Saint Thomas ana-
lyzed temperance and found that it has three parts: *abstinence*, which humanizes our appetites for food and other
pleasure-producing substances; *sobriety*, which humanizes our appetites for intoxicating beverages; and *chastity*, which humanizes our appetite for sexual pleasure
depending on whether we are married, celibate, or single.
"Each of these appetites, when properly satisfied, contributes to the preservation of the individual and of the
human species. Intemperance makes them ends in themselves."[5]

TEMPERANCE—LIVED AND REAL

Temperance is the virtue that helps us strive to become
more human, which itself is something only humans are
concerned about. It is common for authors, experts, and
speakers to talk about the need to deepen our humanity,
and to urge their audiences to "become more human."

An earlier, less verbally inclusive, generation would advise a male to "be a man about it," meaning to act in a given situation with fortitude, temperance, and so forth. Only humans think about being "better than you are," and this is particularly relevant when it comes to the virtue of temperance. This is a distinctively human characteristic.

Certainly no one would advise a dog to "be more like a dog" or an elephant to "deepen your elephantness." Many animals can be taught to perform stunts, to obey, and so forth, but they *already are* all that they can be. We humans, on the other hand, define ourselves by the fact that we constantly fall short of being fully human. The virtue of temperance helps us deepen our humanity and act more like human beings when it comes to our various appetites.

To act with temperance means having a glass or two of wine, or a beer or two, and letting it go at that. To "be a beast about it," in Chesterton's sense, is to be a teetotaler, or to go right on drinking until you make a complete ass of yourself.[6] To "be a beast about it" is to hardly eat at all, or to eat and eat and eat until we are stuffed to the point of illness. Either way, we're a beast. To act with temperance is to enjoy a good meal and call it quits when we have obviously eaten enough. With regard to sex, temperance runs into cultural standards that may, in fact, not be standards at all. It may actually be the lack of standards. When it comes to the human desire for sex, a more detailed discussion is in order.

For a married person, temperance in sex means enjoying sexual pleasure with our spouse as often as it is realistic and responsible. It means reveling in sex at appropriate times; it never means thinking of sex as nasty. It means thinking of sex as sacred and a way to celebrate

the committed love of marriage; it does not mean thinking of sex as an unfortunate bodily activity to be "given
in to" as infrequently as possible.

If anything, the virtue of temperance encourages
spouses to make love frequently. Husbands and wives
need the grace of sex more often, not less often. From the
perspective of a healthy Catholic marital spirituality, this
is a serious matter. In *Familiaris Consortio*, his 1981 ap-
ostolic exhortation on the family, Pope John Paul II wrote:

> Sexuality, by means of which man and woman
> give themselves to one another through the acts
> that are exclusive and proper to spouses, is by no
> means something purely biological, but concerns
> the innermost being of the human person as such
> (no. 11).

Shared sexual pleasure is central to a marital spirituality. Loving sexual intercourse is not just the icing on
the cake for a healthy Catholic marriage; it is the cup
God freely offers couples to nourish marital intimacy and,
once in a while, this love can—and should—result in a
new child. Making love is basic to a couple's relationship
and to their relationship with God. Regular, loving sexual
intercourse is as fundamental to a marital spirituality as
prayer is to the Christian life in general. To put rigid limits on the frequency with which couples may make love,
in the name of the virtue of temperance, is to misunder-
stand the nature of this virtue and stifle God's grace in
marriage.

Because love of God and neighbor cannot be divided,
when husband and wife cultivate loving intimacy with
each other, they also nurture their intimacy with God. To
put this another way, the most physical way husband and

wife nourish their love is also the most spiritual way. Thus, for Catholic couples to welcome, even celebrate, opportunities to *not* make love is self-defeating. This is compatible, however, with a distorted Catholic piety that views celibacy—and verging on the spiritually spectacular—celibate marriages as superior in the eyes of God.

Of course, sex is not the only way spouses express and strengthen their marital bond. There are times, in fact, when the most loving choice a couple can make is not to make love. Still, under normal circumstances, in a healthy marriage, making love is the most complete way husband and wife can ritualize and revitalize their love. Indeed, when spouses make love they celebrate the sacrament of marriage in a special way. Ordinarily couples should no more welcome the chance, in the name of the virtue of temperance, to avoid loving sexual intercourse than they would rejoice at the opportunity to miss Mass on Sunday.

For married couples, the virtue of sexual temperance says "yes" as often as it says "no," and it does not rejoice when sexual abstinence happens more often than making love. Most married couples today find themselves strapped into a hectic schedule of family, work-related and other activities. Exhaustion at the end of the day is, for most couples, the norm rather than the exception. For many, the presence of children further limits the times when they are able to make love. Thus, it's a challenge to find times to make love when both spouses are available and not suffering fatigue.

Most Catholic marriages need more opportunities to make love, not fewer. In marriage today, the virtue of temperance does not require more efforts to avoid sexual pleasure. Rather, temperance requires making the sacrifices necessary to enjoy the grace of making love more often.

For a celibate person, a priest, or a vowed religious, temperance in sex means—that unpopular, culturally unacceptable notion—the *sacrifice* of sexual pleasure for the sake of something else. It does not mean giving up sex because God would rather they gave it up. It means sacrificing sexual pleasure for the sake of the gospel, at the heart of which is love of God—first of all and above all—and love of neighbor; and love of neighbor will happen in truth only if we love God with our whole being.

The celibate abstains from sexual pleasure, but the virtue of temperance helps him or her to do this in order to be a loving person in ways incompatible with the vocation of marriage. Celibacy is for the sake of love and being in relationship with others. As one priest said with a joyful laugh, "I live alone, but I don't have a lonely life. If I had any more 'family' in my life, I think I'd die."

A celibate can "cast a wide net" with his or her loving service for others, while a married person largely limits himself or herself to the love of spouse and children. Of course, the sexual love of spouses is limited absolutely to each other.

The idea of sexual temperance for the single person is a cultural embarrassment in our time. It is practically taken for granted that single people, especially single young adults, are sexually active, indeed, sexually promiscuous. The idea that a single person would "save sex for marriage" is culturally laughable. In particular, the dominant popular culture is blasé about unmarried couples "living together"—a euphemism for what an earlier generation more honestly called "shacking up."

Given the cultural climate, it may be good to focus in more detail on some of the reasons a countercultural sexual temperance should be encouraged for and embraced by single people today. Apart from the obvious conflict between the choice to "cohabit" and the teachings and traditions of the Catholic Church—which cohabiting singles will probably dismiss as irrelevant, anyway—there is more than a little scientific data to support the Church's traditional beliefs. Here is the plain truth: cohabitation is bad for relationships and destructive of the potential for healthy marriages. The virtue of temperance will guide engaged couples to live apart and abstain from sex until after their wedding.

A study conducted by Columbia University and cited in *New Woman* magazine found that "only 26% of women surveyed, and 19% of the men, married the person with whom they were cohabiting."[7] In other words, cohabiting greatly increases the chances that a couple will break up before they marry. If they do marry, however, the couple is not home free. The National Survey of Families and Households reveals that when couples cohabit prior to marriage they have a "50 percent higher disruption (divorce or separation) rate than marriages without premarital cohabitation."[8] Given our already high national average divorce rate of 50 percent, this means that the divorce rate for couples who cohabit before marriage is nearly 75 percent. Therefore, if a couple cohabits prior to marriage, the odds against them having a lasting marriage is about four to one against!

To cohabit prior to marriage is to bring a superficial consumer mentality to one of life's most important decisions. To cohabit prior to marriage is to treat the other person as a mere commodity that needs to be "tried out" or taken for a "test drive" first, much as one would a car. One young man took this attitude so much for granted that he explained he and his fiancée's choice to cohabit by saying, "I wouldn't buy a new pair of shoes without trying them on first, would I?"[9]

The virtue of temperance is vitally important for young single people, because it helps them to see the wisdom of delayed gratification. In a culture that thinks of delayed gratification in any area of life as a horror to avoid at all costs, sexual temperance sounds like something from the Dark Ages. In fact, however, the wisdom of sexual temperance is attested to by many generations of human experience, not to overlook the contemporary studies referred to above.

Considering its own prejudices superior to all this, of course, the contemporary era persists in its narrow-minded conviction that sexual abstinence outside marriage is merely a manifestation of outmoded social, psychological, and religious hangups. The mass entertainment media constantly reinforce the idea that cohabitation is a sign of broad-mindedness and personal liberation, so why should we question it? In the face of significant evidence to the contrary, many young couples actually believe that cohabitation is a superior form of marriage preparation. The virtue of sexual temperance stands neglected in the corner, shaking its head sadly. Is there any hope that the dominant popular culture will ever grow up? Don't bet on it.

The other way in which the virtue of temperance runs up against another wall in our culture is when we apply it to eating. We eat not just to keep body and soul together; rather, we eat for recreational purposes. We eat for emotional reasons as well. We eat when we feel unloved or lonely; we eat when we're bored; some people "graze" all day long. Consequently, countless people are ill and/or overweight. In such a cultural climate the idea of temperance relative to food will sound bizarre in the extreme. Taken seriously, it could put the entire junk-food industry out of business.

Sure, it's fine to say that we are "dieting"; it's even fashionable. But to limit ourselves to three moderate meals a day, with no or few snacks in-between—for spiritual reason or because this is the "virtuous" thing to do or simply because this is what's best—well, we better be ready to have people look at us as if we had two heads. Those who do this had better keep their motives to themselves.

One of the best ways to grow in the virtue of temperance with regard to the appetite for food is to take advantage of the ancient spiritual discipline of fasting. Sure, popular attitudes insist that if you don't have three square meals a day you will begin to starve. But this is nonsense. We need air and water, but it takes about forty days of going without solid food before we begin to starve.[10] Fasting has many values, not least of which is the way it empowers us at other times to stop eating when we should stop eating. In other words, fasting helps us grow in the virtue of temperance.

Begin slowly and easily. Determine to fast one day a month, then do not eat from after lunch one day until lunchtime the next day. That way you only miss two meals. Drink as much water and fruit or vegetable juice as you want, but avoid all solid foods. You will be amazed at what a positive experience fasting can be. You will also find that it is much easier to pray, to be calm, to move more slowly through your day.

The virtue of temperance also applies to the human appetite for intellectual knowledge or understanding. While there is little chance that most North Americans will ever go overboard when it comes to being intellectual, there is a chance that many of us do not develop enough the intellect God gave us. This is particularly true when it comes to our faith.

Many Catholics make do with an understanding of

their religion that hasn't had a growth spurt in decades. The virtue of temperance leads us to turn off the television set for thirty minutes each evening to read a book on a serious religious topic—not just an "inspirational" book, though these have their place, too—but reading that will increase our knowledge and understanding of what it means to be a Catholic in today's world. How many Catholics read a few pages each day from the *Catechism of the Catholic Church*? How many wouldn't miss their favorite television program, but don't make the time to read a good book about Scripture?[11] Why do parish adult-education programs typically attract so few adults? The virtue of temperance with regard to intellectual growth encourages us to integrate our intellect into our faith. It should not be true that someone with a high school or college education still has an elementary school understanding of his or her religion.

CONCLUSION

The virtue of temperance makes it possible for a balanced person to live a balanced life. The virtue of temperance is the virtue of striving every day to live a life that is more fully human because it is governed by a desire for moderation in all things. As temperate persons we do not go overboard with regard to abstinence or with regard to consumption. We enjoy food and drink, sex (if married), work, leisure, and the pleasures of the intellect.

But there comes a moment when the temperate person is eating or drinking and he or she stops eating and drinking; there are times when the temperate married person does not have sex; there is a moment when leisure begins to look like being slothful, so the temperate person gets to work; there comes a time in the day when he or she stops working and enjoys leisure; and the temperate person cultivates the intellect but gladly admits that the intellect will never grasp everything.

In other words, the virtue of temperance is the virtue that keeps us free. The virtue of temperance is the virtue of true freedom—freedom *from* being enslaved to appetites, *freedom to* enjoy them in their proper measure.

❧

VIRTUE

IN A CULTURE OF

SELF-INDULGENCE

I t does not take a career curmudgeon to see that those of us who live in the affluent Western nations have easy lives. Even those who are called "poor" in North America or western Europe are affluent compared to most of the people who live in Haiti, El Salvador, Peru, India, or any of several eastern European countries.

The point is not to cultivate guilt, oh reader. Certainly not. Nor is the point of this book about the Catholic virtues to help us become morally superior to other people. Moral superiority is not the goal of virtue. Rather, the goal of virtue is to actually live in this world as Jesus would live; indeed, to be his presence in our time and our place. The goal of virtue is to be the kind of people who, while admitting that there is precious little we can do for those in places distant to us, try to be people who do not forget those who live in incredible poverty in places like Haiti. The goal is to be the kind of people who, by cultivating the virtues, try to resist the many forms of self-indulgence the dominant popular culture encourages in a thousand seductive ways.

The goal of the Catholic virtues is to become more and more deeply human by becoming more and more authentically disciples of Jesus, the risen Lord. The more deeply human and Christian we become, the more authentically we will live in a culture of self-indulgence. We will not condemn; rather, we will simply follow the directions of the Jesus of John's Gospel when he remarks that his followers will live in the world but according to values and standards that are different from those cherished by the world. This is the goal of the Catholic virtues.

There are no specific directions, no sure-fire way to know that we are being authentically virtuous. There is only the desire that grows in our heart to follow Jesus, to love God with our whole self, to be persons of joy and compassion. This, of course, is a lifelong project, and when we take our last breath and slip through the ever-so-thin veil that divides time from eternity, only then will we be able to abandon the effort to be a more virtuous person. Until then, each and every morning we would do well to make the prayer of Saint Ignatius of Loyola our own prayer:

> Dearest Lord, teach me to be generous.
> Teach me to serve Thee as Thou deservest;
> To give and not to count the cost;
> To fight and not to heed the wounds;
> To toil and not to seek for reward,
> Save that of knowing that
> I do Thy will, O God.

NOTES

Introduction

1. Clifton Fadiman, general editor. *The Little, Brown Book of Anecdotes* (Boston: Little, Brown & Co., 1985), 580.
2. See Richard P. McBrien, general editor. *The HarperCollins Encyclopedia of Catholicism* (San Francisco: HarperSanFrancisco, 1995), 1316–1317.
3. Thomas Merton. *New Seeds of Contemplation* (New York: New Directions, 1972), 35–36.
4. See Mitch and Kathy Finley. *Building Christian Families* (Allen, Texas: Thomas More Publications, 1996).
5. See *The HarperCollins Encyclopedia of Catholicism*, Richard P. McBrien, general editor (San Francisco: HarperSanFrancisco, 1995), 1316.

Chapter One

1. Mary Ann Fatula, O.P., Michael Downey, ed. *The New Dictionary of Catholic Spirituality* (Collegeville, Minnesota: The Liturgical Press, 1993), 379.
2. Fatula, 380.
3. Fatula, 380.
4. Michael L. Cook, S.J. "Faith." *The HarperCollins Encyclopedia of Catholicism* (San Francisco: HarperSanFrancisco, 1995), 515.

5. Henri J. M. Nouwen. *Making All Things New* (San Francisco: HarperSanFrancisco, 1981), 69.
6. Nouwen, 75.
7. Nouwen, 81–82.
8. Nouwen, 88–89.
9. Flannery O'Connor. *The Habit of Being*, selected and edited by Sally Fitzgerald (New York: Farrar, Straus, Giroux, 1979), 422.
10. A recording of this song is available on John Stewart's compact disk, "Punch the Big Guy" (Homecoming Records, P.O. Box 2050, Malibu, CA 90265, [818] 345–6579; e-mail: HcomingRec@aol.com).
11. O'Connor, 354.
12. See Mitch Finley. *The Joy of Being Catholic* (New York: Crossroad Publishing Co., 1997).
13. Frederick Buechner. *Wishful Thinking: A Theological ABC* (San Francisco: Harper & Row, 1973), 25–26.
14. Fatula, 383.
15. Quoted in Tony Castle. *The New Book of Christian Quotations* (New York: Crossroad Publishing Co., 1982), 82.

Chapter Two

1. T. S. Eliot. *T. S. Eliot: The Complete Poems and Plays* (New York: Harcourt, Brace & Co., 1935, 1963), 208–209.
2. Paul Tomasik. "A Legacy of Hope." *Finding Hope: Stories by Teenagers 3*, edited by Carl Koch (Winona, Minnesota: St. Mary's Press, 1998), 16.
3. Tomasik, 17.
4. See Tony Castle. *The New Book of Christian Quotations* (New York: Crossroad Publishing Co., 1989), 117.
5. See Peter Ackroyd. *The Life of Thomas More* (New York: Doubleday, 1998).
6. For a catalog of recordings by John Stewart, write to Homecoming Records, P.O. Box 2050, Malibu, CA 90265–7050.

7. Monika K. Hellwig. "Hope." *The New Dictionary of Catholic Spirituality*, edited by Michael Downey (Collegeville, Minnesota: The Liturgical Press, 1993), 506–507.

8. "Eleanor Boyer's generosity provides inspiration for many," by Rick Hampson. *U.S.A. Today*, April 10–12, 1998.

9. Lou Anne M. Tighe. *Growing in Hope* (Winona, Minnesota: St. Mary's Press, 1998), 17.

10. Thomas Merton. *No Man Is an Island* (New York: Harcourt, Brace & Co., 1955), 14.

11. Gerald G. May, M.D. *Addiction and Grace* (San Francisco: Harper & Row, 1988), 3.

12. May, 5.

13. See Michael J. McManus. *Marriage Savers* (Grand Rapids, Michigan: Zondervan Publishing House, 1993), 140–141. See also David G. Myers, Ph.D., *The Pursuit of Happiness* (New York: Avon Books), 162–163.

14. Merton, 17.

Chapter Three

1. Quoted by Elizabeth Dreyer, "Love," *The New Dictionary of Catholic Spirituality*, Michael Downey, ed. (Collegeville, Minnesota: The Liturgical Press, 1993), 619.

2. Elizabeth Dreyer, in *The New Dictionary of Catholic Spirituality*, Michael Downey, ed. (Collegeville, Minnesota: The Liturgical Press, 1993), 613.

3. See Mitch Finley. *You Are My Beloved: Meditations on God's Steadfast Love* (Williston Park, New York: Resurrection Press, 1999).

4. See Elizabeth Dreyer, "Love," in Michael Downey, ed. *The New Dictionary of Catholic Spirituality*, 614.

5. These excerpts are from Marvin H. Pope. *The Anchor Bible: The Song of Songs* (New York: Doubleday & Co., 1977).

6. See Pope, 517.

7. Eric Fromm. *The Art of Loving* (New York: Harper & Row, 1956). This quotation is taken from the Bantam Books edition (1963), 22. Emphasis is in the original text.
8. Mark Van Doren. *100 Poems* (New York: Hill & Wang, 1967), 11.
9. Merton, 4.
10. Merton, 4.
11. Fyodor Dostoevsky. *The Brothers Karamazov*. Translated by Richard Pevear and Larissa Volokhonsky (New York: Random House/Vintage Classics, 1990), 53.

Chapter Four

1. Clifton Fadiman, general editor. *The Little, Brown Book of Anecdotes* (Boston: Little, Brown & Co., 1985), 124.
2. *Catechism of the Catholic Church* (Libreria Editrice Vaticana/ U.S. Catholic Conference, 1994), n. 1806. Emphasis in original text.
3. *Catechism of the Catholic Church*, n. 1806.
4. Richard P. McBrien. *Catholicism*, New Edition (San Francisco: HarperSanFrancisco, 1994), 975.
5. Quoted in Philip S. Kaufman. *Why You Can Disagree and Remain a Faithful Catholic*, New Revised and Expanded Edition (New York: Crossroad Publishing Co., 1995), 90.
6. The translation of the council document is that given by Richard P. McBrien in his *Catholicism*, New Edition (San Francisco: HarperSanFrancisco, 1994), 972.
7. John Paul II. *Crossing the Threshold of Hope*. Translated from the Italian by Jenny McPhee and Martha McPhee (New York: Knopf, 1994), 191.
8. McBrien, 973–974.

9. See *Rome Has Spoken: A Guide to Forgotten Papal Statements, and How They Have Changed Through the Centuries*, edited by Maureen Fiedler and Linda Rabben (New York: Crossroad, 1998).
10. Pope John Paul II. *Veritatis Splendor* (Washington, D.C.: U.S. Catholic Conference, 1996), n. 64.
11. McBrien, 976.
12. Tony Castle. *The New Book of Christian Quotations* (New York: Crossroad, 1989), 110.
13. McBrien, 980–981
14. *Catechism of the Catholic Church*, n. 1806.
15. Fyodor Dostoevsky. *The Brothers Karamazov*. Translated and annotated by Richard Pevear and Larissa Volokhonsky. (New York: Random House, 1990) 248.
16. Dostoevsky, 251.
17. Dostevsky, 251.

Chapter Five

1. Huston Smith. *The World's Religions: Our Great Wisdom Traditions* (San Francisco: HarperSanFrancisco, 1998, 1991) 288.
2. *Catechism of the Catholic Church* (Libreria Editrice Vaticana/U.S. Catholic Conference, 1994), n. 2439.
3. *Catechism of the Catholic Church*, n. 2266.
4. See Steven M. Nolt. *A History of the Amish* (Intercourse, Pennsylvania: Good Books, 1992), 252–253.
5. Quoted in Nolt, 253.
6. Quoted in Nolt, 253.
7. James J. Megivern. *The Death Penalty: An Historical and Theological Survey* (Mahwah, New Jersey: Paulist Press, 1997), 488.
8. The Business Executives for Economic Justice, *The Buck Stops Here: Perspectives on Stewardship From Business and Professional Managers* (Chicago: ACTA Publications, 1992).

9. The Business Executives for Economic Justice, 4.
10. The Business Executives for Economic Justice, 9.
11. The Business Executives for Economic Justice, 10.
12. The Executives for Economic Justice, 16.
13. See The Business Executives for Economic Justice, 17–18.
14. The Business Executives for Economic Justice, 19.
15. The Business Executives for Economic Justice, 20.
16. *Catechism of the Catholic Church*, no. 2120.
17. *Catechism of the Catholic Church*, no. 2122.

Chapter Six

1. This account was adapted from Boniface Hanley, O.F.M. *Maximilian Kolbe: No Greater Love* (Notre Dame, Indiana: Ave Maria Press, 1982).
2. Jean Porter. "Fortitude," in Richard P. McBrien, general editor, *The HarperCollins Encyclopedia of Catholicism* (San Francisco: HarperSanFrancisco, 1995), 535.
3. See George P. Evans. "Cardinal Virtues," in Michael Downey, ed., *The New Dictionary of Catholic Spirituality* (Collegeville, Minnesota: The Liturgical Press, 1993), 116.
4. Evans, 116.
5. John Stewart. "Across the Milky Way," on *Teresa and the Lost Songs* (Malibu, California: Homecoming Records, compact disk, 1998).
6. Quoted in Peter Gilmour. *Growing in Courage* (Winona, Minnesota: St. Mary's Press, 1998), 22–23.
7. Adapted from Clifton Fadiman, general editor. *The Little, Brown Book of Anecdotes* (Boston: Little, Brown & Co., 1985), 326–327.
8. Adapted from Anthony Castle. *A Treasury of Quips, Quotes & Anecdotes for Preachers and Teachers* (Mystic, Connecticut: Twenty-Third Publications, 1998), 99–100.

9. *Story of a Soul: The Autobiography of St. Thérèse of Lisieux*, translation by John Clarke, O.C.D. (Washington, D.C.: ICS Publications, 1976), 207.

10. Jean Guitton. *The Spiritual Genius of Saint Thérèse of Lisieux*, translated by Felicity Leng (Liguori, Missouri: Liguori/Triumph, 1997), 53.

11. Quoted in Jean Guitton, 56.

12. All of the quotations from Rebbe Nachman are taken from *The Empty Chair: Finding Hope and Joy*, by Rebbe Nachman of Breslov (Woodstock, Vermont: Jewish Lights Publishing, 1994).

13. Therese Johnson Borchard, in her book *Our Catholic Devotions* (New York: Crossroad Publishing Co., 1998), 13, defines devotions as "an organized form of prayer, separate but related to the liturgy, that deepens my personal relationship with God, strengthens my commitment to the Christian community, and leads me to a deeper understanding of the Paschal Mystery, the reality to which my faith continually looks."

14. The author recommends a monthly devotional publication: *Magnificat*, P. O. Box 91, Spencerville, MD 20868-9978. On the Internet: www.magnificat.net

15. Peter Gilmour. *Growing in Courage*, 59.

16. Craig M. Gay. *The Way of the (Modern) World: Or, Why It's Tempting to Live As If God Doesn't Exist* (Grand Rapids, Michigan: Wm. B. Eerdmans, 1998), 2.

Chapter Seven

1. George J. Marlin, et al. *The Quotable Chesterton* (San Francisco: Ignatius Press, 1986), 339–340.

2. See George P. Evans, "The Cardinal Virtues," in Michael P. Downey, general editor. *The New Dictionary of Catholic Spirituality* (Collegeville, Minnesota: The Liturgical Press, 1993), 117.

3. See Richard P. McBrien. *Catholicism*, New Edition (San Francisco: HarperSanFrancisco, 1994), 949.

4. McBrien, 949.
5. McBrien, 949.
6. Obviously, we are not addressing here the disease of alcoholism, in which the only healthy practice is complete abstinence.
7. Quoted by Art A. Bennett, a licensed marriage, family, and child counselor at the Center for Family Development in Bethesda, Maryland, in his column, "Parental Advice." *Catholic Faith & Family*, December 13–19, 1998, p. 13.
8. Quoted by Bennet, p. 13.
9. Anecdote from the author's personal experience.
10. See Richard Foster. *Celebration of Discipline* (San Francisco: HarperSanFrancisco, 1978), 42.
11. If you're looking for such a book, high praise goes to two volumes by the late Father Raymond E. Brown, S.S.: *Responses to 101 Questions on the Bible* (Mahwah, New Jersey: Paulist Press, 1990), and *An Introduction to the New Testament* (New York: Doubleday, 1998).

About the Author

Mitch Finley is a syndicated columnist for the Catholic Sun Columns Service, and he is the author of more than twenty books, including *The Seeker's Guide to Being Catholic; The Joy of Being Catholic; Everybody Has a Guardian Angel...And Other Lasting Lessons I Learned in Catholic Schools; Surprising Mary: Meditations and Prayers on the Mother of Jesus; Your Family in Focus: Appreciating What You Have, Making It Even Better; The Joy of Being a Eucharistic Minister; For Men Only: Strategies for Living Catholic*; and, with his wife, Kathy, *Building Christian Families*. His work has appeared in dozens of religious and secular magazines and newspapers, including *Reader's Digest* and *The Christian Science Monitor*, and has received numerous awards, among which are an Excellence in Writing Award from the American Society of Journalists and Authors, the Thomas More Medal, and seven awards from the Catholic Press Association. He has a B.A. in Religious Studies from Santa Clara University and an M.A. in Theology from Marquette University. He and his wife have three sons.